More Praise for Planting Seeds

"With this wise and lovely book, Thich Nhat Hanh gives caregivers the tools to bring peace into every step of family life. His deceptively simple work with children is transformative and will benefit not only this generation, but generations to come."

SUSAN KAISER GREENLAND
Author of *The Mindful Child*

"Planting Seeds is a treasure, a thoughtful and accessible resource for any teacher or parent."

RICHARD C. BROWN
Contemplative Education Department Chair, Naropa University

"The simple practices in *Planting Seeds* offer each reader the gifts of true peace and happiness. Used regularly, these practices can help us transform our homes, schools, and communities."

AMY SALTZMAN
M.D. Director, Association for Mindfulness in Education

planting seeds

PRACTICING MINDFULNESS
WITH CHILDREN

Thich Nhat Hanh and the
Plum Village Community

Edited by Sister Jewel (Chan Chau Nghiem)

PARALLAX
PRESS

BERKELEY, CALIFORNIA

Note: This book is intended for adults, children, and families of all configurations. It is for people of all physical and mental abilities, including those with limited mobility and/or vision and hearing. Please modify the language to fit the needs of your children. For example, you can add, "move" when the text says "walk," "straighten up" when it says "stand," or "reach toward the earth" when it says "touch the earth." When the text says, "I feel my body lying on the earth," you can add, "I feel my feet touching the earth," or "I am aware of my connection with the earth through the force of gravity" or "through the legs/wheels of my chair."

For more information and additional practices, visit the *Planting Seeds* website: www.plantingseedsbook.org

Parallax Press
P.O. Box 7355
Berkeley, CA 94707
www.parallax.org

Parallax Press is the publishing
division of Unified Buddhist Church, Inc.

Cover and text design by Debbie Berne
Cover and interior illustrations
by Wietske Vriezen

Nhat Hanh, Thich.
  Planting seeds : practicing mindfulness
  with children / Thich Nhat Hanh.
       p. cm.
  Includes bibliographical references.
  ISBN 978-1-935209-80-5
  1. Buddhist education of children.
  2. Meditation—Buddhism—Study and
  teaching. 3. Attention—Religious
  aspects—Buddhism—Study and teaching.
  I. Title.
  BQ5612.N49 2011
  294.3'75083—dc22
                                2010049472

7 / 16

May this book help you plant the seeds of mindfulness in the garden of your own life and in the lives of the children you nurture. And may you, your family, your school, and your community reap a rich harvest of peace, contentment, and togetherness.

contents

PRACTICES

foreword

Of all the things we teach our children, the teaching of mindful presence is one of the most critical yet often ignored in the rush to cover curriculum and manage the task of supervising children. Thich Nhat Hanh draws our attention to a deeper potential in our relationship with our students based on two basic universal human needs: to love and to understand. It is said that the teacher's presence in the classroom is the unwritten curriculum. The transformation of our schools and our society begins with the transformation of ourselves through the practice of cultivating mindful awareness.
—Adele Caemmerer, from Thich Nhat Hanh's retreat for
   teachers in India, 2008

MINDFULNESS is increasingly recognized as an essential educational tool. It develops attention, emotional and cognitive understanding, and bodily awareness and coordination, as well as interpersonal awareness and skills. Most importantly, by diminishing stress, anxiety, and hostility, mindfulness enhances our total well-being, peace, confidence, and joy. Often, the focus of our education system is on competitive performance, with little emphasis on social and emotional learning. It's important that schools teach the key academic skills children need, but it's also critical that schools focus on helping children develop emotional stability and social tolerance. Mindfulness is a powerful tool to help children develop the skills to promote peace in themselves and in the world around them.

Some years ago, the principal of Welham Girls' School in Dehra Dun, India, suggested that I share some mindfulness exercises with the students to help them experience less stress during exam time. I found that simple mindful breathing and walking exercises helped the students find calm and reduced their anxiety. In response to an invitation from the director of the American Embassy School in Delhi, I offered a ten-week mindfulness course for teachers. These teachers continue to meet once a week. Even though they are quite busy, they've made the meetings a priority because they've found that mindfulness is essential to their own and the children's well-being. Cheryl Perkins, a teacher at the American Embassy School with over thirty years of experience, said recently, "I have never used anything in my life that has the calming impact that the mindfulness bell has on the young students in my classroom."

I have been visiting Plum Village since 1989, and each summer Thich Nhat Hanh offers a family retreat. At these retreats, people of all ages practice being aware of who they are, what they are feeling, thinking, speaking, and doing, and what is going on inside and around them. This book and CD are the fruit of decades of development and innovation in the Plum Village community's collective practice with children. Thich Nhat Hanh, along with monastic and lay practitioners, offers insight, stories, and concrete practices from which families, teachers, and anyone working with children can profit. These powerful lessons can be applied at home, in school settings, or in local communities in a way that is meaningful and inviting to children.

This book is a manual for adults to use and share with children. It invites us to practice mindfulness ourselves, so that we can teach from our own experience. If we apply the tools in this book when working with our families and with the children in our communities, both children and adults will benefit from the resulting peace, enhanced communication, and joy. Each person in a community affects the others. If small groups of people practicing mindfulness form within a school or community, a peaceful energy will become pervasive. A feeling of interconnection will start developing among people and with the natural environment. In this holistic and healing atmosphere, each child can develop his or her own unique talents in an openhearted and joyful way.

—Dharmacharya Shantum Seth, Delhi, India, 2010

1

how mindfulness
can help

You cannot transmit wisdom and insight to another person. The seed is already there. A good teacher touches the seed, allowing it to wake up, to sprout, and to grow. —Thich Nhat Hanh

MINDFULNESS HELPS US recognize what is going on in the present moment. When we breathe in mindfully, we are aware of our in-breath. This is mindfulness of breathing. When we enjoy drinking our tea and drink it with full awareness of the present moment, this is mindfulness of drinking. When we walk and become aware of every step we make, that is mindfulness of walking. Practicing mindfulness does not require that we go anywhere else. We can practice mindfulness in our room or on our way from one place to another. We can do the same things we always do—walking, sitting, working, eating, and talking—except we do them with awareness of what we are doing.

Mindfulness is an energy that we can generate for ourselves. We can all breathe in and out mindfully. We can all move mindfully. Every human being has the capacity to be mindful, so it is not something strange. We all have a seed of mindfulness in us. If we keep practicing, that seed will grow strong, and any time we need it, the energy of mindfulness will be there for us.

The practice of mindfulness will increase the quality of our learning and also improve the quality of our life—helping us to handle our suffering and to bring about peace, understanding, and compassion. It can help us improve or restore communication and bring about reconciliation so that we can touch the joy of life. It is important not only to read and speak of mindfulness, but to actually practice it.

When looking at a beautiful sunset, if you are mindful, you can touch the sunset deeply. But if your mind is not concentrated and is distracted by other things—if you're pulled away into the past, or into the future, or by your projects—you're not truly there and can't enjoy the beauty of the sunset. Mindfulness allows you to be fully present in the here and the now in order to enjoy the wonders of life that have the power to heal, transform, and nourish us.

Stopping

According to the Buddha, mindfulness is the source of happiness and joy. We each have a seed of mindfulness, but we usually forget to water it. If we know how to take refuge in our breath, in our steps, then we can touch our seeds of peace and joy and allow them to manifest for our enjoyment. Instead of taking refuge in an abstract notion of God, Buddha, or Allah, we realize that God, Buddha, or Allah can be touched in our breath and our steps.

This sounds easy and everyone can do it, but it takes some training. The practice of stopping is crucial. How do we stop? We stop by being aware of our in-breath, our out-breath, and our steps. Our basic practice is mindful breathing and mindful walking.

If we want to fully enjoy life's gifts, we must practice mindfulness throughout the day, whether we're taking a bath, cooking breakfast for our child, driving to work, or working with children in the classroom. Every step and every breath can be an opportunity for joy and happiness. Life is full of difficulties. If we don't have enough happiness on reserve, we have no means to take care of our despair. With mindfulness, we can preserve our inner joy, so that we can better handle the challenges in our lives. We can create a foundation of freedom, space, and love within ourselves.

Becoming Clear

Before I set up Plum Village, I lived in a hermitage about an hour and a half drive from Paris. It was set on a hill surrounded by woods. One day a family that had fled Vietnam as refugees arrived. The father was looking for a job in Paris, and he asked me to take care of his five-year-old daughter, Thuy, which means "water."

Thuy and another child were staying with me there, and we agreed that when it was time for the evening sitting meditation, they would go to sleep and not talk or play anymore. They would be very quiet as I put on my robe and lit a stick of incense before sitting meditation.

One day, Thuy and a few other girls were playing near the hermitage, and they came in to ask for water to drink. I had some organic apple juice a neighbor had given me. I offered each child a glass. The last serving of apple juice went to Thuy, who did not want to drink it because there was a lot of pulp inside. She left it on the table and went out again to play. About an hour later, she came back very thirsty, looking for water. I pointed to her glass of apple juice and asked, "Why don't you drink that? It's very delicious." She looked at the apple juice and saw that it was now very clear, because after an hour or so, all the pulp had sunk to the bottom. She was very happy to drink it.

Then she asked me why the apple juice had become clear, and I answered that it had been practicing sitting meditation for an hour. And she understood! Because we left the glass there for one hour, it kept still and became clear. She said, "Now I understand why you practice sitting meditation—you want to be clear." I said, "Yes, you understand what sitting meditation means. If you know how to sit, how to put yourself in a stable physical position, if you know how to handle your in-breath and out-breath, then after some time, you become peaceful and clear." That is why we like to do sitting meditation every day. We imitate the glass of apple juice, or the apple juice imitates us!

MIND IN A JAR*

> MATERIALS: mini bell and inviter, clear vase of water, stirrer, different colors of sand—or different kinds of beans and whole grains that will slowly sink in water, like rice, millet, or steel-cut oats (Try it out for yourself first, because some float and don't sink to the bottom. Dry sesame seeds float, but if you soak them overnight they should sink.)

Suggested guiding words are in *italics*. Answers that children have shared with us are in [*brackets*].

Bring out a large, clear vase filled with water and set it in the middle of the circle of children. Set out several containers of colored sand.

The vase of water is our mind, and the different colors of sand are our thoughts and feelings. What kinds of thoughts do you have when waking up?

[*Looking forward to seeing friends at school, wanting to sleep longer, hunger.*]

Each of you can pick a color of sand that feels right for your feelings or thoughts, and then sprinkle a handful into the vase.

Ask another child to begin stirring the water so that the sand swirls around.

And what thoughts do you have when you go to school, in the afternoon, and in the evening before bed? The children may share feelings of joy, sadness, irritation, anger, peace, and sleepiness that arise in them throughout the day. For each feeling, they continue to add their sand to the colorful, swirling water.

The child who is stirring can stir the sand even faster. *This is how our minds are when we are in a hurry, stressed, angry, or upset. Can you see things clearly in this state? Is it a pleasant state? Name some examples of when you feel this way.*

[*When my mom yells at me, when I'm scared, when I get into a fight with my brother.*]

---

*This is an adaptation of the original exercise in *Peaceful Piggy Meditation*, by Kerry Lee MacLean (Park Ridge, IL: Albert Whitman & Co., 2004).

Now sound the bell and have the child stop stirring. *Let's breathe with the bell and observe all the sand as it slowly settles to the bottom of the jar.* The children often find this quite relaxing.

This is what happens to our minds when we meditate, when we are mindful of our body and of our breathing. What is the water like now?

[*It's clear. It's peaceful.*]

The thoughts and feelings can still be there in our minds but rest peacefully at the bottom, because we know how to return to our breathing to calm them.

We can also choose which kind of feelings and thoughts we want to stir up in our mind. There are times when we can look into our unhappy thoughts and feelings in order to understand them better. Or we can bring up those thoughts that make us happy, like kindness, compassion, and forgiveness. It's important to be aware of our thoughts so that we can guide them in the direction we want to go, rather than being guided by them.

Mindfulness is being aware and alert. To me being mindful is when you look deep to see what others are going through. It is important to water good seeds so that people grow and develop good qualities and become better people.

RIYAAZ, age 11
American Embassy School, Delhi

The Benefits of Practicing Mindfulness with Children*

Teachers may often ask their students to "pay attention," but they may not teach them how to do so. The practice of mindfulness teaches students how to pay attention, and this way of paying attention enhances both academic and social-emotional learning.

Mindfulness is a very effective response to stress and enhances the neurological process called "executive function," or the ability to organize tasks, manage time, set priorities, and make decisions. Children—including those

---

*Adapted from Dr. Amy Saltzman's *Mindfulness—A Guide for Teachers*. Saltzman, Amy. "Teachers Guide | The Buddha." PBS: Public Broadcasting Service. 07 July 2010. www.pbs.org/thebuddha/teachers-guide

diagnosed with stress-related disorders—can benefit from learning to focus their attention, becoming less reactive, and more compassionate with themselves and others.

MINDFUL CHILDREN*

are better able to focus and concentrate

experience increased calm

experience decreased stress and anxiety

experience improved impulse control

have increased self-awareness

find skillful ways to respond to difficult emotions

are empathetic and understanding of others

have natural conflict resolution skills

MINDFUL TEACHERS**

have an awareness of themselves and are attuned to their students

are responsive to students' needs

maintain emotional balance

nurture a learning community where students flourish academically, emotionally, and socially

thrive professionally and personally

know how to manage and reduce stress

have healthy relationships at work and at home

---

* Testimonials from "Teachers and Students Who Have Received Mindful Schools Instruction." *Mindful Schools: Using Mindfulness to Teach Children to Be Emotionally Aware, Empathetic, and Mindful of Their Thoughts and Actions.* 09 Aug. 2010. www.mindfulschools.org

** From *Mindful Teaching and Teaching Mindfulness*, by Deborah Schoeberlein (Somerville, MA: Wisdom Publications, 2009).

2
practicing with children in plum village

I very much count on young people to learn things that are not taught at school, such as mindful breathing, mindful walking, learning how to look deeply, and learning how to take care of anger. —Thich Nhat Hanh

EVERY SUMMER, hundreds of young people come to our retreat center at Plum Village in southwest France to participate in a family retreat. Some fifty different nationalities are often represented. The children speak English, French, German, Spanish, and Hebrew, among other languages, and they enjoy each other a lot. I like walking with the children, and they always join me during walking meditation. We climb the hill, we go to the woods, and we enjoy our togetherness. Halfway through walking meditation we sit down and silently enjoy the beauty of summer. The children always sit around me very quietly and joyfully, and it makes me very happy. Walking meditation is one of the things I enjoy the most, especially when children walk with me.

It's amazing that children, even the very young ones, also enjoy silence. This is not an oppressive silence, but rather one that is eloquent and powerful. In Plum Village, we call it Noble Silence, because it can heal, nourish, and bring us peace. The children know how to walk mindfully in silence, how to breathe mindfully and enjoy their breathing. Together we generate the energy of peace and joy. None of us wants to watch TV or play electronic games, and we survive just fine!

If the children enjoy Plum Village, it is not because we are well organized. We are not well organized in Plum Village! The children enjoy Plum Village because they learn to practice mindful walking, mindful sitting, and mindful breathing. Together we create a very powerful energy of peace, mindfulness, and joy. What the children profit from the most in Plum Village are not the Dharma talks or other formal teachings, but the stillness and peace generated by the community.

sharing . . . .

PRACTICING AS A FAMILY

by Sister Cuc Nghiem and Sister Anh Nghiem, Plum Village, France

Families who come on retreat can learn and practice together as a family. Children are welcome at any of the activities, but if they prefer, they can also go outside and play. The way we do everything throughout the entire day is *itself* the retreat. We offer many mindfulness tools that help adults and children to stop and return to the present moment. In our centers, we hear the sound of bells ringing many times a day. Every time we hear one of these mindfulness bells, we all stop—we stop moving, stop working, stop talking. Even the children learn to stop running and playing. Everyone returns to their breathing to connect body and mind together in the present moment.

When parents stop, the children stop too. The whole village stops. Imagine five or six hundred people all stopping to breathe and relax body and mind. The children are carried by this flow of practice because everybody is doing the same thing. When moments like these occur frequently throughout the day, the practice becomes

the very air that we all breathe. It becomes our way of life. There aren't separate adults' and children's practices; the essence of the practice is the same for everyone. By learning and cultivating mindfulness together on retreat, families learn to adapt these practices to their everyday life at home.

Watering Seeds of Beauty and Goodness

Children have a need and a great capacity for spiritual learning and growth. When spiritual practice is communicated simply and directly to them, the children experience it as fun and helpful. The Children's Program brings together all the children and creates a sense of belonging and connection among them. It is a space where they can experience being in a unique atmosphere of compassion and joy that schools may not always provide.

Sometimes people hand over their children to us as if saying, "Here, please fix them." But there is no plan to fix the children. We offer them space to be who they want to be. We share some of the practices. But more than anything, we allow them to be who they are. If they are bored, they learn to practice, "Breathing in, I'm bored; breathing out, it's okay to be bored." We allow them space to feel and accept their feelings as they are.

The Children's Program is about taking care, sharing, and relating to children from a place of mindfulness, compassion, and wisdom.

A Room of Peace: Setting up the Children's Space on Retreat

How much we enjoy being in a certain place depends very much on the energy that is generated within it. A room can be well decorated but feel cold and unfriendly; another can lack color and furniture but feel simple, spacious, and comfortable. Together, we help create the

atmosphere. A children's room should feel like a place of refuge for the children and for those who work with them. Any child should feel free to go there, even outside of activity time. A children's room can offer arts and crafts, games, and storytelling, but another important element should also be offered: peace.

A special corner with a few precious objects on an altar—a small statue of a Buddha or a *bodhisattva*, an incense holder, one or two candles, some flowers or a small plant—can make the space feel more sacred. When children and their parents enter the children's room on the very first day of the retreat, we invite them to leave their shoes outside. Once they are seated and settled in the room, we invite them to close their eyes and imagine they have just entered a zone very different from the one outside the room. We ask them to imagine they have just stepped inside a place in which time suddenly slows down, slowing them down, too. They become less hurried, less scattered, and more centered. They take slower steps; their hearing is more alert; their speech is quieter; and they don't need to shout. Perhaps they would like to stand before the altar and offer a bow, or simply look at the objects on the altar. Sometimes we share a simple song to bring the energy of the group together.

Lit incense can make the atmosphere calm and special. We offer incense before the beginning of the first session and last session of the day. Of course, the room can also be a place to play games, run, and shout, once everyone has already known its peace. We bring the children back to this peace at least twice a day, at the first and last gathering of each day.

Many of the elements of the children's room on a retreat can be adapted to school and home settings. Children can perform a small ritual when entering the classroom to help them return to awareness of body, of breathing, and to touch the peace inside. Instead of taking off their shoes or bowing, they can stretch and take three deep breaths before sitting down. Children can keep a mindfulness pebble on their desk, hold it, and breathe three times. Everyone can sing a calming song together.

Ideas for Preparing the Children's Room

Put a welcome sign or hang a welcome banner at the entrance with the names of all the children on it.

- Display a poster of the Two Promises (*on page 133*) at the beginning of the retreat, so children see it often.
- Post beautiful drawings of Pebble Meditation to help children remember the four steps (*on page 76*).
- Post the Food Contemplations Before Eating (*on page 142*).
- Cover the bottom half of one or more walls with paper that children can decorate throughout the retreat as an ongoing, collective mural.

sharing. . . . .

BEING AIMLESS WITH CHILDREN

by Brother Phap Dung, Deer Park Monastery, USA

There is no fine line between "practice" and "not practice." In fact, it is best and most effective when we share ourselves with the children without the idea that we are sharing the practice. Our presence and ordinariness are fundamental in making any activity enjoyable. How we respond, our quality of being, our warmth and kindness, is what most benefits the children. With ease and effortlessness, we can share with them the wonders and joy in a particular activity.

Simply Being Present

Our basic practice is to be mindfully present for ourselves and for those around us. Mindfulness helps us recognize what is happening inside us and outside us. We can sense the children and the atmosphere by just relaxing into the present moment. In the United States, the children sometimes call this "hanging out," "chilling," or "kicking it." This wonderful way of being has at its core the practice of aimlessness, of being comfortable and at ease with the present situation.

We enter the children's space and merge with their circle, without demanding anything or forcing things to happen. There's a lot of space and time, and no rush. And then, from a smile, a laugh, a sharing, a slow opening, things begin to flow and move naturally.

There are no hard and fast rules for being with the children; no particular method, except perhaps a sense of awe or intense curiosity. It is as if we are about to go on a journey to a place we've never been before, with all of our attention and all of our energy in a state of alertness, ready to explore.

To hang out, then, is to simply *be* with a child. It is to let the child reveal to us who she or he is: how he talks, her voice, how he moves about, what she wants to play, his smile, her face with all its expressions, what he dreams, her total being. It is being open to accept what is being offered and improvise with it, so as to be playful yet caring. Let our interactions be a moving meditation.

Togetherness and Diversity

Sometimes we divide the children into smaller groups by age or language because they can get comfortable quickly in these more familiar groups. However, some children feel a larger sense of acceptance and inclusiveness when we gather in a large circle of children of different ages and languages. It's a lesson in itself for the children to experience differences in culture and age. It's also important for them to see the inclusion of "the difficult ones" or "the different ones" and to see how the staff handles these differences and embraces all cultures, languages, and ages.

Spontaneous Play and Teaching

Planning an activity is wonderful, but being spontaneous can also be enriching. We plan so that there is room for spontaneity. We are aware of the children's energy level and adjust the activity appropriately. For example, when the children have a lot of energy, we try an outdoor activity, although sometimes Deep Relaxation (also called Napping Meditation by the kids) works, because their excess energy can actually mean they are tired. When they are calm and attentive, we may do something indoors such as artwork or storytelling. There is no formula for spontaneous activity. Attention and flexibility are crucial for allowing rich moments of interaction, creativity, and growth to arise.

Challenging Moments: Personal Stories

In being with children, we each have important moments of learning and connection that stay with us for the rest of our lives. They make working with children meaningful and fulfilling. They teach us so much about ourselves, our perceptions, and our vulnerability.

Sometimes we think that as adults we always need to be in control and look like we know what we're doing. We think we should never let the children see that we're vulnerable or that we've lost our authority. But sometimes miracles can happen when as adults we reveal our truest feelings and weaknesses right in the midst of the present moment. We can be true to ourselves and to what is happening, letting go of our ideas of how things should be, embracing the present moment, and trusting that the truth of the moment is okay as it is. When this true embrace and acceptance occurs, something changes in the children and in the collective environment.

BETRAYED

by Brother Phap Dung, Deer Park Monastery, USA

One time, when I was teaching Pebble Meditation to a room of forty or fifty children, things did not go as planned. The children were of mixed ages from toddlers to older teens, with a group of four to five young boys who seemed bored with the sharing and more interested in distracting me. I was close to each one of them, had cared for and played with them separately when they would come visit the monastery with their families. It was very hard for me because as a group they were interrupting me as soon as I shared. The disruption affected the other kids as well. Sweat formed on my forehead and everyone in the room realized we had a difficult situation. All were waiting to see if someone could restore calm. Because I was close to the children, I didn't want my monastic brother who was also present to remove any of them from the room. Yet I felt betrayed by these young boys. They were embarrassing me in front of everyone, and I felt hurt and angry.

As I raised the pebble for the third time and said, "This first pebble represents a flower, our capacity for 'freshness' inside," the distraction became unbearable. With sweat still running down my face, I dropped my arms, closed my eyes, and began to follow my breathing. I let go. The situation was beyond control. The room quieted and everyone waited for me to speak again. I felt the heat inside of me slowly cooling as I recognized my anger and my hurt. I said, "Breathing in, I am hurt. Breathing out, it is okay to be hurt." My monastic sister invited the bell. "Breathing in, I feel betrayed by my friends. Breathing out, I smile to them with love and understanding." I continued with this type of guided meditation for a while, acknowledging my feelings and especially acknowledging what was happening in the room. Everyone knew what was happening, but no one knew what to do.

When the situation was acknowledged with respect, something changed. In Thay's words, we had called the situation by its "true name." The boys were recognized. They got their attention from the group, but they also got something else—the recognition that they were interrupting the group. I felt that they understood this because their body movements began to change. They straightened up; they quieted down; and they began to listen and pay attention to what was happening in the group.

That morning session turned out to be about dealing with our emotions and challenges, rather than about pebble meditation. We asked the children how they felt when other kids were creating a distraction and how they deal with themselves when they are annoyed or upset. It turned out to be an enriching experience for all of us.

Reflecting back now, I see that we should have foreseen the need to split the group into two and deal with the boys earlier. I also see that I held on to a notion about how that morning should have been. I resisted what was happening in the present moment and forcefully tried to create my idea of how things should be. I didn't respect my feelings. We could have asked the boys to leave the room and everything might have gone as planned. But this experience was a gift for me, because I learned that the transformation that happens in my mind when I sincerely recognize and respect my present moment as it truly is— whether that moment contains sadness, anger, or other feelings—also happens in the collective mind of the group.

WHITE MOTH BODHISATTVA

by Brother Phap Dung, Deer Park Monastery, USA

One evening, when the children were singing and dancing in a circle, a white moth entered the circle and danced with us. She landed on the carpet beside me and I knelt down to say hello to her. Just as I said, "How wonderful, children! A beautiful white moth has joined us with her song," a young boy moved forward quickly and stomped on the moth violently many times. A few other boys joined him. One girl screamed in horror. Other children were in shock, and my brothers and sisters embraced and consoled them. I picked up the dead moth and took it outside to return it back to the earth. When I came back, the room was silent. I sat in the middle of the circle, closed my eyes, and followed my breathing for a few minutes. My sister invited the bell.

I began to pray for the moth and to express our regret for our unskillfulness. "Dear white moth, please forgive us for not recognizing your beauty, your gift to us, your sacrifice to our ignorance, our violence, and our unskillfulness. We pray that you are now in a peaceful place, and that your pain in leaving us was not too great. We are in pain now for what has occurred. You came to us to share your wonder, your dance, and your love for the children. Yet we could not see. We were blinded by our excitement, our habit of killing small living beings, and our inability to care for all beings. No one person is to blame for this act, for it is an action we are all responsible for. We promise to do better next time. We promise to respect life in all its forms—plants and animals, even small bugs and insects. We promise not to kill and let our violent energy take us over and destroy what is beautiful and good in this world." We then invited each child to share their feelings, express their hurt, speak to the moth, and ask for forgiveness for our actions. "Thank you, dear moth, for being with us." "We are sorry for hurting you and killing you." "We hope you are okay." As each child shared their thoughts and the boys shared their regret, the energy of the room began to change and the young girls who had been crying because of the incident felt comforted.

This experience opened up the discussion. We shared about the mosquitoes, worms, butterflies, and bugs that are in our lives, how we should treat them, and that they want to live just like we do. It turned out to be one of the deepest and most real discussions that I have ever had about the Two Promises with children of that age. Thank you, Moth Bodhisattva, for your gift and sacrifice.

THE HUG

by Sister Anh Nghiem, Blue Cliff Monastery, USA

James was a young boy of seven. He had two close friends, Paul and Yves, who were seven and eight, and the three of them were very tight. The other four children in the group were girls. Whatever the planned activity might be, the girls listened to me, but James and his friends rebelled silently and were unresponsive to my ideas and suggestions.

If the children and I went for a walk, James and his friends ran from us, playing their own games. If we were inside the children's room doing some arts and crafts, the three of them would be outside running around the building. If we were skit-playing, they were playing something else. The entire week continued like this.

I wasn't quite sure what to do. I didn't want to shout or force them to do anything, but I let them know they were always welcome to join in with the group.

On the last evening of the week, we had a Rose Ceremony for honoring our parents. After the ceremony James's mother, with James a little behind her, came up and asked me if James could give me a hug. I was more than surprised. He looked so shy and vulnerable as he approached me, and no longer like the leader of the pack he had been. I felt a deep happiness as I embraced him, and I was conscious not to hold him too close or too tight. After three breaths James continued to hold on to me. His hug became tighter; he wouldn't let go.

I realized then that James had taken in everything that had happened in the past week. He had sensed and received everything. It wasn't the activities we did or the practices we learned. What James received was acceptance in our attitude toward him and his friends. How we are and the way we are with the children is what is imprinted in their hearts.

Planting Seeds

SINGING A STORY

by Anonymous, Children's Program Staff

Sitting with a group of six-year-olds, I began a story. During the story, one child started to make singing noises and continued for a while. I stopped speaking and he continued to sing. Gently, I asked him, "Is it okay if I continue with the story?" He offered a rather strange non-reply, and I continued the story while he continued this song-like speaking. Suddenly I found myself adapting to *his* voice and letting his voice guide mine. The story took on colors and emotions I had never felt before. We were all entranced. The young boy continued like this through more than an hour of storytelling. The teachers were fascinated. I later learned that the boy is autistic and had never listened to any story or performance for more than ten minutes. I still thank him silently for the lesson he taught me that day.

PLANTING SEEDS OF PEACE

by Sister Chan Dinh Nghiem

In the first summer retreats that we had at the New Hamlet in Plum Village, I took care of the French children. Every day I learned so much, and I was deeply nourished by them. They had lots of energy and it was tiring to take care of them, but it was rewarding because they received my love easily and in return they gave me love. The fruits, the consequences, of what I did were immediate. The children told me how happy they were even though we only had a few simple toys for them. They said they were happy because in Plum Village their parents were so much quieter and gentler than they were at home. They loved being in Plum Village because they saw how their parents transformed.

Each day the children surprised me. They would fidget and move around during the Dharma talk, but when I asked them questions after the talk, they knew everything; they had heard everything. When they returned home with their parents, they were the ones who maintained the practice and remembered it longer than their parents. They're like blank sheets of paper. When I think back to the things I received in Buddhist temples as a girl, I see that I remember every little thing. When I took care of kids in Plum Village, they were a bell of mindfulness for me. They really helped me to practice. Anything I said, anything I did, they remembered for years. I only want to draw beautiful things on those blank sheets of paper.

I remember one day the children were too noisy and agitated and I was extremely tired. After just one week, I had lost my voice. They were shouting, jumping, and doing whatever they liked. I was so exhausted that suddenly I lay down like a dead person. Then the girls calmed the boys down, saying, "Be quiet, look at Sister Dinh Nghiem. She's so tired because we are too noisy." They calmed themselves down, and I didn't need to use control. Because there was love between us and they saw that I was tired, they tried to help me.

I have learned that the most important thing to transmit to the children is our way of being. The children are very sensitive. They don't live by their intellect; they live by their feelings. So our presence, calmness, gentleness, and peace are the most important things we can offer them. Therefore, we need to really practice in order to have these things to transmit to them.

The best way to transmit the teachings is to tell the children stories and then have them reenact the tales. They all love to act in skits. They also love the practices of Beginning Anew and Tea Meditation with their parents. It is wonderful to include parents in these activities and practices. Every year, these sessions have been successful and very moving.

As the children come back year after year, I see how they grow up. Last summer, I was really happy because they formed a Sangha and kept in touch with each other during the year. In the next Summer Retreat, they came together to welcome the young newcomers and make them comfortable. They were so happy together that, even though they were teenagers, they still wanted to be in the children's group!

Through these young people, I can already see the future of Buddhism in the West. The practice is so natural to them now. When they grow up, mindfulness will seem normal. Since they started learning as children, the practice has become their life. They aren't getting stuck on the intellectual level. Because they understand the essence of the teachings, I know they will be creative and find ways to make the practice more appropriate to the West.

PLUM VILLAGE: A PLACE FOR CHILDREN

by Michele Hill, Hawaii, USA

This summer I traveled halfway around the world, from Hawaii to France, to participate in the simple retreat life of Plum Village. Perhaps the most impressive thing to me there was the role of children. The kind of Zen that many of us have practiced over the last decade or so in the West has essentially been that of a modified monastic schedule. Rarely, if ever, have we had visitors with children attend an entire *sesshin*, or training period. Those who may have come for a brief visit have had to rely on their own resources to deal with the issue of child care, often sharing with other parents.

As more of our Sangha members have children, the separation between a lay family life and this essentially monastic practice has increased dramatically. At Plum Village, I found that children are not only present, they are the center of the community. They are given regular responsibilities in the meditation hall such as inviting the bell, leading tea meditation, and participating in ceremonies. They participate in everything, and people pay attention to them quite naturally. At several group discussions, Thay raised the issue of including children in practice. Children seem to have a natural love of ceremonies, rituals, songs, and games. Parents of small children often say that it is the child who remembers to hold hands before dinner, who recognizes the beauty of a small ritual like bowing on entering the meditation hall.

Thay said that if you cannot explain what you are doing to your children, maybe it isn't real. Children must be included and understand what you are doing if it is to be real Buddhism. Thay feels that children can understand the most profound Buddhist ideas, which at the core are very simple and straightforward, such as, "You are me and I am you," "to understand is to love," and "when a finger is hurt the whole hand suffers."

Thay said, "We have to find a practice that is pleasant for children. It is very important, for if we can't include the children, something is lacking. When children are included, the practice will be pleasant for the parents as well."

These words made a deep impression on me. How often had I heard my friends express feelings of being torn between being with their children and meditating. Working parents whose jobs take them away from home so much are reluctant to leave their children again in the evenings or on weekends. I have noticed that while a few families in our Sangha have tried, most have abandoned the effort. It seems to me that creating a practice that includes children will solve a multitude of problems and enrich the experience for all of us. Thay states, "Practice is impossible without the support of children. Without this, it is an escape from family and society."

3
cultivating our own mindfulness

TO SUCCESSFULLY SHARE mindfulness with children, you must first practice it yourself. Your presence, your calm, and your peace are the biggest gifts you can offer to young people. When you are solid, happy, and full of compassion, you will naturally know how to create a happy family or school environment, and how to water the positive qualities in your children, other family members, students, and your colleagues at work. What every really good school has in common is the quality of its teachers. To be a good teacher or parent, you have to know yourself and take good care of yourself. You need a practice that helps you deal intelligently and compassionately with your emotions, with your suffering, so that you can compassionately address the suffering in your children, students, and colleagues.

We all carry wounds in us that we received as children, and taking the path of healing these wounds makes it much easier for us to relate to and understand the children in our life. Whatever we haven't transformed, we're likely to pass on to our children and to our students. Our suffering will become their suffering. This is why practicing mindfulness in our daily lives is so important. It is not just to avoid burnout; mindfulness allows us to transform in the depths of our consciousness. This chapter on caring for yourself may be the most important one in the book. If you are not at peace, how can you impart peace to your children and students?

The First Step: Taking Care of Ourselves

We have to learn how to take care of ourselves throughout the day, while walking, sitting, eating, or brushing our teeth. Our home is made up of our body, feelings, emotions, perceptions, and consciousness. The territory of our home is large, and we are the monarch who is responsible for it. We should know how to go home to ourselves and take care of our body and our mind. Mindfulness can help. Suppose we have pain, tension, and stress in our bodies. The first step is to go back to our body and take care of it. We can do this by taking a moment to be still and say:

Breathing in, I am aware of my whole body.
Breathing out, I let go of all the tension in my body.

After we know how to take care of our body, we learn how to take care of our feelings and our emotions. With mindfulness we can bring up feelings of joy and happiness. When a strong emotion arises, we should know how to take care of it. We can repeat this short practice poem, called a *gatha*, to help us care for these emotions.

Breathing in, I am aware of the painful feeling in me.
Breathing out, I am embracing it with tenderness.

We don't try to cover up the feeling by consuming. Many of us would rather avoid our pain, so we try and drown the feeling with movies, the Internet, books, alcohol, food, shopping, and conversations so that we don't have to feel our suffering. Ultimately, this only makes the situation worse.

The Buddha said that nothing can survive without food. If our pain, our sorrow, our fears are still there, it's because we keep feeding them. Once we have recognized and embraced our pain, our sorrow, our fear, and found some relief, we can continue to practice looking deeply into the nature of our pain to recognize its roots. We can recognize what kind of nutrient has brought about our ill-being, fear, and depression.

If we suffer from depression, it means we have lived and consumed in such a way that has made depression possible. The Buddha said that if we look deeply into what has come to be, namely our ill-being, and recognize the source of nutrient that has brought it about, we are already on the path of emancipation.

Our children may consume a lot of violence, fear, and craving. When they watch television, they witness thousands of acts of violence, which makes the seeds of violence, craving, and fear in them grow. Now there is a lot of violence in young people, and they don't know how to handle their emotions and their suffering. We parents and educators should be able to help them to handle their fear, anger, and violence. The population of France isn't very large, yet every year more than twelve thousand young people commit suicide. They are victims of strong emotions like anger, fear, and despair. In school they're not taught how to handle these strong emotions. It is very important that we parents and teachers learn how to handle our emotions so we can help young people at home and in our class do the same. We have consumed in such a way that our fear, anger, and despair have grown very big, so mindful consumption is the answer and is our practice. We should consume in such a way that prevents the negative elements in us from being nourished.

Love also cannot survive without food. If we don't feed our love, it will die someday. This is why it is very important to recognize what kind of nutrients we need in order to nourish the positive things in us. We can consume only those things that develop our understanding, our compassion, and our love.

Here are practices you can apply in your daily life to strengthen the energy of mindfulness, reduce tension, and nurture joy. You can start slowly, applying just one practice in your daily life and gradually increasing the number. You don't have to practice mindfulness perfectly before you can begin to share it with children. Already when you begin to practice, you start to transform, and the fruit of your transformation—even if it is still quite small—will be of benefit to your children, your students, or to the young people you work with.

ESTABLISHING A DAILY MINDFULNESS ROUTINE

It's very helpful to set aside five to ten minutes every day for mindful breathing, either in the morning or in the evening. Try to practice at the same time every day in a place that supports calm and concentration. You can sit on a chair or on a cushion on the floor. Sit comfortably, with your back straight, but relaxed. You can close your eyes or keep them half open. Simply follow your in- and out-breath, giving your attention to the whole of your in-breath and then the whole of your out-breath. You may also use the guided meditation below.

GUIDED MEDITATION, JOY OF MEDITATION AS NOURISHMENT*

This guided meditation can be practiced in the sitting position, or while walking, or lying in bed before sleep. Practice each exercise for at least ten in-and out-breaths, using the keywords that summarize each exercise to help to focus your mind on the exercise. If your mind drifts off, just gently bring it back to the breathing and the keywords.

1	*Breathing in, I know I am breathing in.*	IN
	Breathing out, I know I am breathing out.	OUT
2	*Breathing in, my breath grows deep.*	DEEP
	Breathing out, my breath goes slowly.	SLOW
3	*Aware of my body, I breathe in.*	AWARE OF BODY
	Relaxing my body, I breathe out.	RELAXING BODY
4	*Calming my body, I breathe in.*	CALMING BODY
	Caring for my body, I breathe out.	CARING FOR BODY

* For more guided meditations, see www.plantingseedsbook.org and *The Blooming of a Lotus: Guided Meditation Exercises for Healing and Transformation* by Thich Nhat Hanh (Boston, MA: Beacon Press, 1993).

5	*Smiling to my body, I breathe in.*	SMILING TO BODY
	Easing my body, I breathe out.	EASING BODY
6	*Smiling to my body, I breathe in.*	SMILING TO BODY
	Releasing the tension in my body, I breathe out.	RELEASING TENSION
7	*Feeling joyful to be alive, I breathe in.*	FEELING JOYFUL
	Feeling happy, I breathe out.	FEELING HAPPY
8	*Dwelling in the present moment, I breathe in.*	BEING PRESENT
	Enjoying the present moment, I breathe out.	ENJOYING
9	*Aware of my stable posture, I breathe in.*	STABLE POSTURE
	Enjoying the stability, I breathe out.	ENJOYING

ONE ACTION IN MINDFULNESS

In addition to practicing mindful breathing each day, you can choose to be fully aware of one action every day. Every time I climb the stairs, I enjoy every step. Breathing in, I make a step and smile. Breathing out, I enjoy it. I have made a treaty with the stairs in my hermitage that if I miss enjoying a step, if I take a step without mindfulness, then I go back and try again! If you like, you can also sign a peace treaty with your stairs, with a part of the route from your house to the bus stop, or from your work to your car.

You can also choose other activities to enjoy deeply: perhaps brushing your teeth in full awareness, opening and closing doors, turning on the light, or driving. Whenever you do this activity, do not allow your mind to be elsewhere, lost in your thinking; bring one hundred percent of your attention to that act and make it a meditation.

BREATHING POEMS*

Gathas are short mindfulness poems we can use to bring more awakening into our daily life. We can recite one line with our in-breath and the next line with

---

★ There are more poems on the *Planting Seeds* website: www.plantingseedsbook.org

our out-breath. Be creative and make up your own poems for the activities you want to do more mindfully.

Waking Up

Waking up this morning, I smile.
Twenty-four brand new hours are before me.
I vow to live them mindfully
and to look upon all beings with eyes of compassion and love

Correcting/Reading Students' work

Breathing in, I am in touch with the effort my student is making to learn.
Breathing out, I encourage and guide with clarity, skillfulness, and compassion.

SMILING MEDITATION

It is important not to forget our own smile and the power it has. Our smile can bring much joy and relaxation to us and to others around us at the same time. Smiling is a kind of mouth yoga. When we smile, it releases the tension in our face. Others notice it, even strangers, and are likely to smile back. By smiling, we initiate a wonderful chain reaction, touching the joy in anyone we encounter. A smile is an ambassador of goodwill. As you smile, take a few in- and out-breaths.

Breathing in, I smile.
Breathing out, I relax and touch joy.

LAZY DAY

In all of the Plum Village practice centers around the world, there is a Lazy Day once a week with no scheduled activities except meals. When we know how to live deeply, our Lazy Day can be the most delicious day of the week. Being lazy does not mean we don't practice, but simply that we practice on our own.

There is no bell calling us to activities, there is no schedule, and everyone is free to do what he or she wants to do, including sleeping or reading. The Lazy Day is a very sacred day, similar to the Sabbath in other traditions. On Lazy Day, we try to be as lazy as possible. It's not so easy to be lazy because we have the habit of always doing something.

If we want, we can rest in a hammock. We can practice walking meditation or sitting meditation on our own, or we can organize a picnic or an outing. We can turn off the phone and the computer and give ourselves space and time to do things we cannot do on other days, like taking a long walk, writing a poem, making a cup of tea and drinking it slowly while we contemplate the sky, or inviting a friend to sit silently with us while we enjoy each other's company. Whatever we do, we do in mindfulness, because that is the best way to deeply enjoy it.

Not doing anything, just enjoying ourselves and whatever is around us, is a very deep practice, because we all have an energy within us that constantly pushes us to do this or that. We cannot sit or lie still and enjoy ourselves or enjoy the beautiful sky. If we aren't doing something, we can't stand it. We have to practice in order to transform this kind of habit energy that is always pushing us to do something, to say something. If we are capable of doing that, our Lazy Day will be rewarding. If we can't take a whole day, we can set aside half a day or a few hours each week. Every Lazy Day can offer us different things to do—not exactly to do but to *be*.

The Second Step: Taking Care of Our Relationships

After a few weeks of practicing to take good care of ourselves, we will begin to feel much better. Then we can make the second step of going to our partner, our friend, or our coworker in order to take care of him. We have to take care of ourselves before we can love and take care of someone else. We can help our loved ones take care of their suffering, but not before we can take care of our own.

When we take better care of ourselves, we can more clearly see that those we love are also suffering. They have their own difficulties. Reaching out to our partner, our co-parent, our colleagues will help strengthen our own skills as parents, teachers, and caretakers.

Many of us have lost our capacity for listening and using loving speech. We feel very lonely, even in our own family. When communication is cut off, we all suffer. When no one listens to us or understands us, we become like a bomb ready to explode.

Deep, compassionate listening can heal the situation. Sometimes only ten minutes of listening deeply can transform us and bring a smile back to our lips. We also need to train ourselves to use loving speech so that we can restore harmony, love, and happiness.

We have lost our capacity to say things calmly and to speak with kindness. We get irritated too easily. Perhaps both you and the other person, who may be your friend or your partner, have been suffering in the past several years. Both of you seem to have lost your capacity for listening deeply to each other, with compassion. Because there is so much pain, suffering, and violence in you, it is difficult to listen with compassion and patience anymore. Because the blocks of suffering are too great, even if you want to use loving speech, it has become too difficult. You intend to speak calmly, but as you tell the other person what is in your heart, you become bitter and judgmental. This makes it more difficult for her to continue listening to you. Learning to listen calmly and compassionately and to use peaceful, loving speech are very important. These two instruments are necessary to restore communication.

After practicing mindful breathing and looking deeply into the situation to recognize that you also have contributed to creating the difficult situation between you, you can go to her. With your full presence, you tell her in loving language, "Darling, I know that you have suffered a lot in the last three or four years. I am also partly responsible for that suffering. I did not understand your suffering and your difficulties enough, so I have made many mistakes in my speech and actions. I did not intend to make you suffer. I did and said those things out of unskillfulness. I only wanted to make you happy, but because I did not know enough about your suffering, your difficulties, I have made many mistakes. I really want to listen to what is in your heart. Please tell me of your suffering, your difficulties, your deepest desire. Please help me so that we can be happy again." If you can speak with that kind of language, the door of that person's heart will open again.

When the other person shares with you, tell yourself that the only purpose of listening is to allow him to find relief from his suffering. No matter what he says, you will listen. In a relationship, we can have wrong perceptions of each other every day. When you listen to your beloved, you recognize how many wrong perceptions he has of you, and you may recognize that you also have wrong perceptions about him. But you just continue to listen. You don't react. Later on you can offer information that can remedy his misperceptions, but not now. Maybe in several days or a week you can share some information to help the other person alter his perceptions, but not too much at one time because he may not be able to take it all in. Share information little by little so the other person will have the capacity to receive and correct his wrong perceptions.

Even if the other person expresses a lot of bitterness, misperceptions, judgments, and condemnation, you still continue to listen with compassion. To keep compassion alive while you listen is an art, and to do so you have to remember to practice mindfulness. One hour of listening like this can already help the person suffer much less. Compassion protects you so that what the other person says will not touch the seed of irritation or anger in you. You listen like the bodhisattva, or great being, of compassion. That is the technique. The bodhisattva of compassion is not somewhere in the sky. The bodhisattva of compassion is in every cell of your body. If you know how to touch her, she will express herself and stay in your heart during the time of deep listening.

When you put all your heart into it, you can listen even better than a psychotherapist. If your beloved one suffers, there is no way you can be happy, so invest one hundred percent of yourself into the act of listening. Maintain compassion alive in your heart during the whole time of listening. If you feel you are not strong enough to listen, don't force yourself. Tell your beloved, "Darling, I am not in good shape today. Could we sit together another time so that I can listen to you with all my heart?" Then you can go out and practice mindful walking and mindful breathing to get more strength to succeed in your practice of deep listening.

If we are not mindful in our relationships, we can say or do things that create suffering in the other person. It may be just a small grain of suffering that we think is not worth talking about, but thinking this way is very dangerous. Day after day, the suffering continues to grow, and then one day, you can no longer look at the other person with happiness anymore. In the beginning your love is so beautiful. You only want to look at your beloved every day. Just looking at her brings you a lot of pleasure. But now when you look at her, you don't feel happy anymore, and instead you may both look at the television to avoid looking at each other. This is a failure in the relationship. We can always do something to help each other rediscover our love.

The best way to encourage the other person to use loving speech is to practice it ourselves. When we practice loving speech, we benefit; we experience happiness, and slowly the other person recognizes the power and effectiveness of loving speech.

Confronting a situation of injustice or oppression, you can also use loving speech because it is the only kind of speech that can get through to the other person or group. If you insult, reproach, or condemn someone, they will not listen to you. You lose your energy and you don't get anywhere.

Once you succeed in transforming your anger, fear, and sorrow, you can help your beloved. In the past you may have tried but did not succeed because you had not yet changed yourself. Now that you have changed yourself, you can inspire your beloved to do the same. Then, when you go home or meet your friend you can share with them the joy and the difficulties in the work of educating the young people. The other person is your supporter, encouraging and sharing in your work as an educator.

BEGINNING ANEW

To begin anew is to look deeply and honestly at ourselves, our past actions, speech, and thoughts, and to create a fresh beginning within ourselves and in our relationships with others. We practice Beginning Anew to clear our mind and keep our practice fresh. When a difficulty arises in our relationship and one of us feels resentment or hurt, we know it is time to begin anew.

Beginning Anew helps us develop our kind speech and compassionate listening because it is a practice of recognition and appreciation of the positive elements within our community. Recognizing others' positive traits allows us to see our own good qualities as well. Along with these good traits, we each have areas of weakness, such as talking in anger or being caught in our misperceptions. As in a garden, when we "water the flowers" of loving kindness and compassion in each other, we also diminish the weeds of anger, jealousy, and misperception.

We can practice Beginning Anew every week. We may like to have a vase of flowers in front of us to help us remember our freshness. The practice has three parts: flower watering, expressing regrets, and expressing hurts and difficulties. This practice can prevent feelings of hurt from building up over the weeks and helps make the situation safe for everyone in the community.*

1. We begin with flower watering.
When we speak, our words reflect the freshness and beauty of the flowers between us. During flower watering, the speaker acknowledges the wholesome, wonderful qualities of the others. It is not flattery; we always speak the truth.

---

* A worksheet is on www.plantingseedsbook.org

Everyone has strong points we can see when we are aware. Also, we do not interrupt while another is speaking. We are allowed as much time as we need, and everyone else practices deep listening.

We should not underestimate the first step of flower watering. When we can sincerely recognize the beautiful qualities of other people, it is very difficult to hold on to our feelings of anger and resentment. We will naturally soften and our perspective will become wider and more inclusive of the whole reality. When we are no longer caught in misperceptions, irritation, and judgment, we can easily find the way to reconcile ourselves with others in our community or family. The essence of this practice is to restore love and understanding between members of the community. The form that the practice takes needs to be appropriate to the situation and people involved. It is always helpful to consult with others who have more experience in the practice and have gone through similar difficulties in order to benefit from their experiences.*

2. In the second step, we express regret for anything we have done to hurt others.
It does not take more than one thoughtless phrase to hurt someone. The practice of Beginning Anew is an opportunity for us to recall some regret from earlier in the week and undo it.

3. In the third step, we express ways in which others have hurt us.
Loving speech is crucial. We want to heal our relations and the community, not harm them. We speak frankly, but we do not want to be destructive. Listening meditation is an important part of the practice. When we sit among a circle of friends who are all practicing deep listening, our speech becomes more beautiful and more constructive. We never blame or argue.

In this final part of the practice, compassionate listening is crucial. We listen to another's hurts and difficulties with the willingness to relieve the

---

* To find a Sangha or practice center in your area in the tradition of Thich Nhat Hanh, visit www.iamhome.org

suffering of the other person, not to judge or argue with him. We listen with all our attention. Even if we hear something that is not true, we continue to listen deeply so the other person can express his pain and release the tension within. If we reply to him or correct him, the practice will not bear fruit. We just listen. If we need to tell the other person that his perception was not correct, we can do that a few days later, privately and calmly. Then, at the next Beginning Anew session, he may be the person who rectifies the error, and we will not have to say anything. We can close the practice with a song or by breathing mindfully together.

PEACE TREATY AND PEACE NOTE

Suppose someone we care about says something unkind to us, and we feel hurt. If we reply right away, we risk making the situation worse. Another option is to breathe in and out to calm ourselves, and when we are calm enough, say, "Dear, what you just said hurt me. I would like to look deeply into it, and I would like you to look deeply into it, also. Then we can make an appointment for some time later in the week to look at it together." One person looking at the roots of our suffering is good; two people looking together is even better.

We may be at war with ourselves inside, hurting our bodies with drugs or alcohol. Now we have the opportunity to sign a treaty with our bodies, our feelings, and our emotions. Once we make a peace treaty with them, we can have some peace, and we begin to reconcile with our beloved. If there is a war inside us, it is very easy to start a war with our beloved, not to mention with our enemies. If our beloved is our enemy, how can we hope to have peace in our relationships, our country, and in the world?

We all have the seed of wisdom in us. We know that punishing leads us nowhere, and yet we are always trying to punish someone. When our beloved says or does something that makes us suffer, we want to punish her, because we believe that by punishing her we will get some relief. There are times when we are lucid and we know that this is childish and ignorant. When we make our beloved ones suffer, they may also try to get some relief by punishing us in turn, resulting in an escalation of punishment.

The treaty suggests Friday as the night for discussion, though you can pick any night. You make an appointment for Friday because if you are still hurt, it may be too risky to begin discussing it before. You might say things that will make the situation worse. Until Friday evening, you can practice looking deeply into the nature of your suffering, and the other person can too. Before Friday night, one or both of you may see the root of the problem and be able to come to the other and apologize. Then, on Friday night, you can simply have a cup of tea together and enjoy each other. This is the practice of meditation. Meditation is to calm ourselves and to look deeply into the nature of our suffering.

If the suffering has not been transformed by Friday evening, practice the art of listening like the Bodhisattva Avalokiteshvara: one person expressing himself, while the other person listens deeply. When you speak, share what is deep in your heart using loving speech—the kind of speech the other person can understand and accept. While listening, you know that your listening must be of a good quality to relieve the other person of his suffering. When you're able to resolve your conflict on Friday evening, then you have Saturday and Sunday to enjoy being together.

The Peace Treaty and Peace Note are two tools to help us heal anger and hurt in our relationships. When we sign the Peace Treaty, we are making peace not just with the other person, but within ourselves. We do not need the other person to sign it for it to be effective. Even if just one person begins practicing according to it, the situation can change a great deal. At retreats for couples in our centers, we have a special ceremony in which the Peace Treaty is read and individuals or couples can come up to formally sign it in front of the whole community.

It is better to do more than just read the Peace Treaty. Try to sign it in front of others, or even in the presence of family and community. It solidifies your commitment and invites the Sangha's support. The text of the Peace Treaty and Peace Note are on the Planting Seeds website.

WRITING A LOVE LETTER

If we have difficulties with someone in our life, we might spend some time alone and write a letter to her. We can write the letter to someone we see every day or, just as effectively, to someone we have not seen for years. Many people have found this practice helpful when writing to a family member who is no longer living. The work of reconciliation is a great offering we can make to ourselves, our beloved ones, and our ancestors. We reconcile with the aspects of our mother and father inside of us, forgiving them and accepting them as they are. If we are estranged from them, this may lead us to discover a skillful way to reconcile with them. It is never too late to bring peace and healing into our family.

Give yourself at least a few hours to write a letter using loving speech. While you write the letter, practice looking deeply into the nature of your relationship. Why has communication been difficult? Why has happiness not been possible?

Your letter might
1   Acknowledge the other's suffering
2   Acknowledge your part in the other's suffering
3   Ask for help from the other
4   Acknowledge that you cannot be happy if the other is not happy
5   Promise to stop making the other suffer

Writing a love letter does not mean we cannot tell the truth; we can tell the whole truth but in the language of loving kindness. Before writing we have to practice looking deeply into the mind, the consciousness of the other in order to see his difficulties and suffering. If we show that we understand his suffering and difficulties, he will want to read our letter. People like to read love letters, not hate letters. With this kind of language we will be able to communicate all our insight, all our ideas to our beloved.

I have a disciple who became a monk. His father was furious because he expected his son to become a doctor and earn a lot of money to support the family. But the son felt he could help more people as a monk than as a doctor. His father was so angry that he would not answer his son's telephone calls and or any of his letters. With my help, one day the son wrote a love letter. He wrote something like this: "Father, in my community the brothers keep telling me I have many qualities like perseverance, considerateness, and loving kindness. In the beginning, I did not believe that I had these qualities, but they kept telling me I did, so finally I accepted that it is true. When I look deeply, I see that these qualities have come from you. Without you, how could I have these qualities? I feel very grateful to you, to my mother, and to my ancestors. Because of the wonderful qualities that my parents and ancestors have transmitted to me, my brothers in the monastic community like and appreciate me. I write this letter in order to express my gratitude to you, Father, and to my ancestors. I now want very much to learn more about my ancestors. I know very little about my grandfather and great grandfather. Father, can you tell me more about them so I can learn more about my roots?"

After reading this letter, his father answered with a ten-page letter, and communication between father and son was completely restored. One letter can create a miracle. The practice of loving speech is wonderful. It can touch the hearts of people. It can restore communication, bring back harmony, and dissipate misunderstanding. Just practicing it for a few minutes, you can already see the effects.

The Third Step: Bringing Mindfulness to Our Community

Once we have been able to take care of ourselves and have helped colleagues and loved ones to do the same, we can try to bring the practice of peace and mindfulness to our class, our school, and our community. This needs to be done in partnership with friends or colleagues, not alone. With mindfulness, we can recognize and learn to address the suffering of our students and colleagues. We have to listen deeply to them and help them listen to each other deeply. We can practice loving speech and deep listening to restore good communication within our school community, and this will improve the quality of teaching and learning. Our happiness will support us in the work of sharing the fruit of our teaching and learning with other communities in the field of education. Only when we are successful in beginning to bring mindfulness into our own community of teaching and learning can we help change the system in the whole country, which is the fourth step.

In the school setting, this means we also have to organize ourselves as a community of educators. The principal can play a very important role in organizing the school so that educators can come together regularly, to learn and help each other. It is essential that we set up a community of educators, because it will generate more solidity, freedom, and happiness, and this is the basis of our work. We all need a Sangha to nourish our practice and keep it alive. Every day we should get the nourishment and the healing we need from our own practice and the practice of our Sangha.

We do this not only for our own sake, but also for the sake of many others in our community who need our freshness and solidity. We must know our limits and not take on more work than we can realistically accomplish. Even if the need around us is huge, we have to preserve ourselves. We need time to nourish and restore ourselves.

If you want to continue for a long time, you have to take care of yourself. Sometimes it is not easy because the situation is very demanding, but if you lose yourself, if you burn out, those who need you will suffer. It is not a question of how much you can do. The question is, can you continue to do it every day?

Without this solidity and happiness generated by our practice, we have nothing to offer. It is not simply a matter of doing, of acting; it's a matter of *being.* Being peace is the ground of doing peace. If there is no peace in being there will be no peace in doing. To be peace is the foundation of peaceful action.

Q & A

QUESTION: *Our school seems to operate under the philosophy that more is better. Although the school implements many valuable programs, it continues to ask teachers and students to do more. I've tried to question the real value in doing too many worthwhile tasks, but I am beginning to feel that I am alone in a vision of a more relaxed, peaceful daily experience. I am also fearful that administrators view me as a complainer and troublemaker. How do I reconcile this for myself? Do I continue to work at this frenetic pace and remain silent about what this is teaching our students and what it is doing to teachers? Short of walking away from this school, how can I be true to my commitment of mindfulness while working in this environment?*

THAY: You may like to write a love letter to your headmaster, to the board. They have their suffering and difficulties, and in the beginning of the love letter you should recognize their suffering and difficulties. Maybe you have not seen their suffering or their difficulties. Maybe they are expected by their superiors to do what they want you to do. You may have some wrong perceptions of them, so you should not be too sure that they don't have problems, difficulties, or pressures of their own. They may be under a lot of pressure. When you have understood their situation, you can begin to write a love letter with no blame or judgment. You can fully express your insight, your ideas, and your needs. You may like to share the letter with one or two colleagues to receive their insights before you give it to the administrator.

sharing . . . .

EVERYDAY MINDFULNESS FOR A TEACHER
by Tineke Spruytenburg, the Netherlands

I teach autistic six- and seven-year-olds. It is the most challenging job I have ever had! Without a daily practice of mindfulness I would not be able to do it! Before I leave the house, I practice sitting meditation for at least twenty minutes. En route to school, I observe my mind running into the day and bring my mind back to my body.

What is most challenging is taking care of the emotions that come up while working with the kids. Many of our students act out when they are fearful or confused without being aware of the consequences—like the time a seven-year-old kicked me so hard I had to go see a doctor.

Looking back on this event, I know that it was the emotional pain and not the physical pain that made my leg feel so weak. Now, I take a time-out for myself when something like this happens. If possible, I leave the classroom and practice walking meditation in the hallway or go to the nearest toilet to sit and follow my breathing for a few minutes.

Fear, lack of understanding, and problems with concentration are everyday challenges for our students with autism. We practice mindfulness of breathing a few times a week, usually before or after we do some physical exercises in the classroom, like yoga. I also introduce mindful eating, without mentioning the word, to help them concentrate on their food. We eat in silence to give them a break from the information and sensorial stimuli they receive during the lessons. Most of the children cherish this moment of withdrawal and calm, so maintaining the silence is not very difficult as long as I set the example. When I am distracted and look around or do some work, the silence is easily broken.

I have also introduced them to mindful walking. We have to walk a few minutes to get to one of our classes. Although our walking is structured and orderly, the children are easily distracted by what is inside and around them. One day I gave them a task: "From here to the school gate, I invite you to concentrate completely on how your feet are moving, how it feels to put them on the ground and lift them again for the following step. Do not think about anything; just observe how you are walking. When we arrive, we will talk about your experiences." The whole group responded to the invitation. When we arrived, a boy shared that it felt like eating something with all your attention, very calming. Another child said she would use this way of walking when her mind became noisy. These moments of silence help children and adults regain their energy and create a group energy of togetherness and concentration.

sharing. . . . .

BUILDING A SCHOOL SANGHA

by an anonymous teacher, Germany

When I first learned about mindfulness in Plum Village in 2005, I felt that it would be a great help in my job as a high school teacher. But how? In the beginning, I rarely brought the practice into the classroom explicitly.

Slowly, the inner foundation of my work started to change. It turned from a hollow pressure to meet work demands into something healthy and beautiful. If things don't work according to plan, I now have an inner shelter where I can take refuge and ask myself, What would be the way of love and understanding here? No need to fight, no need to control anybody else, no need to complain about the flaws of others. These are collective habit energies that are very strong in our school system and in me. Now, if I sit down and share with the Buddha or with the Sangha, I can return to myself, breathe, and tell myself that it's okay. I'm doing my best, and I also deserve patience, love, and understanding.

I read *Keeping the Peace: Mindfulness and Public Service,* a book by Thay on how to bring the practice into public service. It contains a sentence I will never forget: "If you want to bring the benefits of the practice to those you serve, it is very helpful to build a community of co-practitioners among colleagues in order to support your aspiration." Although in the beginning I was quite shy to share about my spiritual path with people from school, Thay's advice encouraged me not to keep it a secret. Once in a while I would mention that I had been to a retreat or to the Sangha. With time, I realized that some people were quite interested, so I would share a little bit about the practice and how I benefited from it. I never got a negative response. When I felt that it was welcome, I invited them to visit a meeting of our local Sangha. Without doing much to make it happen, I realized that Thay's suggestion might come true.

This year, three colleagues joined me at a weeklong course for teachers at the European Institute of Applied Buddhism in Waldbrol, Germany, and after our return home we started a school Sangha.[*] Here is how we have been practicing together since then:

- We meet every second week for one hour and fifteen minutes. After practicing sitting meditation for ten or fifteen minutes, we each share how we are doing, what preoccupies us, our joyful experiences, and difficulties at school. We close the meeting with a discussion about the practices we will do for the next two weeks and school Sangha issues. We water each other's flower, expressing mutual appreciation, and sing several songs.
- We focus on a different practice for each day of the week: breathing, walking, eating, smiling, or accepting. During the day we can look at each other and see each other

[*]See www.eiab.eu for more information.

practicing, or a glance from another teacher might remind us to come back to the day's practice.

• We place a ceramic jar on the windowsill inside the teachers' room, and everyone contributes some small cards with gathas or inspiring quotes by Thay. Whenever we need Sangha energy, we can pick one from the jar or pass one to a friend. It's very beautiful.

Another source of great joy is our recent second body system, or buddy system (see page 115). We try to support our second body by smiling, asking about her, sticking a message in her school mailbox, or placing a flower on her desk. Often we feel inspired to pass on what we have received, so the energy truly circulates through the Sangha. It is inspiring to see how everybody creates new ways to apply the practice to our job with the students. We also find it much easier to offer the practice to students when we feel the support of the group.

4

mindful breathing and listening to the bell

THE SOUND OF THE BELL is the voice of the Buddha within, because there is a Buddha within every one of us. The Buddha represents our capacity to be mindful, compassionate, and understanding. Listening to the sound of the bell is listening to the voice of understanding and compassion within us, calling us home, reminding us to be more at peace with ourselves and with the world. When we are distracted, we need the voice of the Buddha within calling us back, saying, "Come home, come home to yourself. Don't lose yourself in anger, in frustration."

When we're away from our true home for a long time, we long to return to it. In our true home, we feel at peace. We feel we don't have to run anywhere; we feel we are free of problems. We can relax and be ourselves. It's wonderful to be the way you are. You are already what you want to become. You don't need to be someone or something else. Look at the apple tree. It's wonderful for the apple tree just to be the apple tree. It doesn't have to become something else. It's wonderful that I am myself, that you are yourself. We only need to let ourselves be what we already are, and enjoy ourselves just as we are. That feeling, that realization, is our true home. Each of us has a true home inside.

Our true home always calls to us, day and night, in a very clear voice. It keeps sending us waves of love and concern, but they don't reach us because we are so busy. When we hear the sound of the bell, we let go of everything—talking, thinking, playing, singing, being with friends—and we go back to our true home.

When we listen to the sound of the bell, the reason we don't talk or think or do anything is because we are listening to the voice of a person we love and respect a lot. Just stand quietly and listen with all your heart. If there are three sounds, listen and breathe deeply during the entire period. As you concentrate, you can say to yourself, "Breathing in, I feel fine; breathing out, I feel happy." What is the use of breathing and practicing if it doesn't help you feel well and happy? The deepest desire in each of us is to be happy and to bring happiness to the people and other beings around us.

Breathing with the Mindfulness Bell

MATERIALS: mini bell and inviter, CD player

For younger children, you might like to choose one or two activities per session from the following section. You could share one activity at the beginning of your session with the children and one again at the end to reinforce the lesson. Or, you could introduce a different bell or breathing exercise in the first five to ten minutes of every session. Suggested guiding words are in *italics*. Answers that the children have shared with us are in [*brackets*].

STOPPING WITH THE BELL

In our first session with the children, in schools or on retreats, we often introduce them to the practice of listening to and inviting the bell. Holding up the mini bell, ask, *Do you know what this is? Do any of you have one at home? What do we do when we hear the sound of the bell?*

The sound of the bell is the voice of the Buddha, or the voice of someone who loves us very much and wants us to be happy and peaceful.* *When we hear the bell, we stop what we are doing and saying, and just breathe. We have a chance to rest, to take a break, to enjoy ourselves. We are only aware of our in-breath and out-breath.*

Invite the bell a few times for them to practice this.

Now we are going to practice stopping with the bell. Feel free to walk or move around the room and when you hear the bell, we will all stop and breathe three times. Then continue moving, but stop and breathe each time you hear the bell.

IDENTIFYING THE IN-BREATH AND OUT-BREATH

To help you really get to know your breathing, hold a finger horizontally right under your nose to feel your exhalation. What does the out-breath feel like? Warm, moist? Can you feel it? What does the in-breath feel like? Cool? We breathe all the time, but we are usually not aware of it and we take it for granted. But breathing is so important! What would happen to us if we couldn't breathe?

Now put your hands on your belly—what happens when you breathe in and when you breathe out?

[*Our tummy rises when we breathe in and falls when we breathe out.*]

Feel this rhythm for a few moments in silence. How do you feel when you just pay attention to your breathing?

[*More peaceful and calm.*]

Learning to notice my breathing has helped me in difficult moments (give an example if you can). *Breathing with awareness the way we have been doing can help you to calm down when you get upset or nervous, and can also help you focus better in class and when taking a test. Any time we are aware of our breathing, whatever we experience in the moment improves—if we are happy, we become happier, and if we*

---

* If it makes you feel more comfortable, instead of "Buddha" you can say "the energy of understanding and compassion," or "unconditional love," or "our true nature, our true goodness," or "God, Jesus, or Allah."

TRACK 1

I Follow My Breath

are suffering, mindful breathing helps us to suffer less, to calm down, and to see things more clearly. Play the song "I Follow My Breath." Afterward, you can ask the children, *What did you learn from the song? Were some of the suggestions in it already familiar to you?*

AWARENESS OF THE LENGTH OF OUR IN-BREATH AND OUT-BREATH

Now let us notice how many seconds our in-breath lasts and how many seconds our out-breath lasts. There is no right number. Each of us breathes according to our own lung capacity, and we want to allow our breathing to be natural. It may be that the out-breath is a little bit longer than the in-breath. Let the in-breath stay the same. When you breathe out, try breathing out all the air from your lungs, pulling in your abdomen and allowing your out-breath to become a little bit longer. But don't force it. It should be pleasant. If you enjoy lengthening the out-breath, you can also try it with the in-breath. How does it feel to breathe longer on the in- and out-breath?

You could bring a clock with a second hand so that the children can time their in-breaths and out-breaths. Ask them to share how long their breaths are. They could write the length on a piece of paper or come up and write it on the board.

COUNTING THE BREATH WITH THE BELL

Now let us continue in this style of slightly lengthening our breathing, and begin to count our breaths. We will count how many breaths we take during one sound of the bell. I will invite the bell and you can count each out-breath until you can no longer hear the bell's resonance. Then raise your hand. It may be easier if you close your eyes, but you can also keep them open.

Wake up the bell and invite one sound. When the sound has totally faded, say, *Show me on your fingers how many out-breaths you counted during the sound of the bell. There is no right number; each of us breathes differently.*

Now we will see if we can count each out-breath, all the way up to 10. Breathe in, and when you breathe out, count "one." Just count on the out-breath.

When the children are finished, you can ask, *Is it easy or hard to pay attention to each breath for ten breaths? Did anyone get distracted and lose count? It's okay to get distracted. If you notice you have lost count, don't worry; just start again. Let's try once more.*

GATHA FOR LISTENING TO THE BELL

There is a gatha, or poem, for listening to the bell:

Breathing in, we say: "Listen, Listen."
Breathing out, we say: "This wonderful sound is bringing me
back to my true home."

I will invite the bell, and then we will recite the gatha out loud together three times. This helps the children get used to saying the gatha to themselves when they breathe in and out three times after each sound of the bell. Teach them the gatha as a song, "Gatha for Listening to the Bell."

TRACK 2

Gatha for Listening
to the Bell

What is our true home? We all have a beautiful, safe place inside of us where we can always go that is full of peace. The bridge that takes us to this place within us is our breathing. That's why the bell is so important, because it helps us breathe and go back to this true home, this island of peace and clarity inside of us. When have you experienced being in your true home? When do you feel peaceful, calm, and clear? What other things besides the bell can help you go back to your true home?

TRACK 3

The Island Within

If you like, you can teach them the song, "The Island Within."

You can also have the children write down the gatha and decorate it with images of what it is like in their true home. They can also use images from the "The Island Within" song, such as trees, sunshine, streams, and birds. Or, you can prepare a large poster with the gatha on it, and all the children can decorate it with images of their true home. Hang up the poster, or the children's gatha drawings, so that they can always be reminded of how to practice when they hear the bell.

LEARNING TO INVITE THE BELL

If there are children in the group who already know how to invite the bell, encourage them to share and model the practice for the others. Ask the children to sit upright and beautifully like a Buddha. They can sit on a chair or on the floor, cross-legged or kneeling, keeping their back straight and relaxed.

We only invite the bell when we are calm and peaceful, because the sound of the bell reflects our mind. We can help others to be peaceful only when we are also peaceful. We can recite this poem before we invite the bell. As you breathe in, say to yourself:

Body, speech, and mind in perfect oneness.

This means you have concentration. As you breathe out, recite the second line,

I send my heart along with the sound of this bell.

This means you send your love to the world. With your next in-breath, recite:

May the hearers awaken from forgetfulness

Forgetfulness is the opposite of mindfulness, and the sound of the bell helps us to be mindful. Hearing the voice of the Buddha, we come back to the present moment. With your next out-breath, recite,

And transcend the path of anxiety and sorrow.

It's okay if you forget the gatha as you ring the bell, but try your best to remember it.

You can also teach the children another version of the above poem:

Breathing in: I am really here, with my mind and body together.
Breathing out: I want this sound of the bell to help others feel calm and happy.

Or an even simpler version:

Breathing in, I am calm. Breathing out, I smile.

If you use the shorter version, repeat it twice. It's good if the children can breathe in and out at least two times before picking up the bell. If you have time, you can also ask the children to write their own short poems for listening to and inviting the bell, and then to really practice using them whenever they hear or invite the bell.

When you practice breathing in and out while reciting the gatha, your mind and body become united. You are concentrated, and you have the beautiful wish that everyone who hears this bell feels no sorrow, anger, or anxiety, and that they enjoy breathing and smiling. Breathing in and out two times with the gatha, you are now qualified to be a bell master. You have enough peace, calm, and concentration. Even if you are still very young, just six or seven years old, you can be a good bell master.

We say, "inviting the bell to sound," not "striking" or "hitting" the bell because we always treat the bell with respect, as we know it can help many people. Then, we join our palms and bow to express our respect to the bell and also to show the unity of our mind and body. We pick up the bell and place it in the palm of one hand that remains flat and outstretched. With the other hand we pick up the inviter and wake up the bell. We wake up the bell to let others know a full sound is coming, so that they can come to a stop and enjoy the sound and the stopping without being surprised. After making the wake-up sound, we breathe in and out one time before inviting a full sound of the bell. This gives everyone time to finish what they are doing and come to a stop. The full sound should be strong and clear. If we mistakenly invite the bell too softly, we can invite a stronger sound straight away. Then we enjoy three in-breaths and out-breaths. We place the bell down and bow.

Ask all the children to try inviting the bell once. The children really enjoy this, and they are often very quiet as they breathe three times in respect for each child's sound of the bell. They often forget to wake up the bell, so you need to remind them. Sometimes they're nervous and don't invite it properly. Gently encourage them to try again. You can also ask them to share how they feel when they invite the bell. You may like to point out that it is common for adults to breathe more slowly than children, so when children invite the bell for adults, they can give a few extra seconds. This way, the adults also have time to breathe in and out three times.

Once they have learned how to invite the bell, you can ask the children to invite the bell whenever you begin and end sessions together. Remind them that they need to be calm and breathe in and out two times before they invite the bell. You can also encourage them to have a bell at home so that whenever the atmosphere in the family is tense, angry, or distracted, they can invite the bell and remind their parents and siblings to breathe. Many children do use the bell in this way at home.

Many teachers have also successfully used the bell in their classrooms. You can have the children take turns inviting the bell throughout the class period, especially when the atmosphere is not very peaceful. If you don't have a bell, you can develop another sound. Some classes have one student clap every fifteen minutes, and everyone stops and comes back to their breathing. Or the class might come up with another sound that they like.

LISTENING TO OUR BUDDHA NATURE

Did you know the Buddha calls to us? Today we will listen to see if we can hear the Buddha calling us. Listen, I think he is calling us now!

Recite the gatha for inviting the bell out loud, and invite one sound of the bell.

Did you hear the Buddha call to us? When we hear a bell, we are hearing the Buddha calling us! That is why we stop whatever we are doing and show respect to the Buddha in the bell. We stop our moving. We stop our thinking. We stop our talking and we listen to the beautiful sound of the Buddha. It is not the Buddha from a long time ago who is calling us; it is the Buddha inside ourselves; it is our Buddha nature. We smile when we hear the call. We breathe in and we say to the Buddha inside ourselves—to our Buddha nature—"I listen. I listen." Then we breathe out and say to our Buddha nature, "This wonderful sound brings me back to my true, calm, loving self."

Sometimes the Buddha is a bell. Sometimes the Buddha is a bird singing. Sometimes the Buddha is a baby crying or a telephone ringing. There may be other sounds that make you feel peaceful and happy. Can you think of other sounds that the Buddha inside you might use to call you back to your Buddha nature?

[My dad calling me; laughter; an alarm clock; thunder; the wind in the trees; a rooster crowing; the sound of a river; an airplane flying over my house; a horn honking; my cat meowing.]

These, too, are the voice of the Buddha, the sound of awakening, and these sounds can help us come back to the place of calm and peace within us.

TRACK 4

Listen, Listen

At this point you could play the song "Listen, Listen." *Which sounds did you notice in this song? What are the different sounds that we hear throughout the day and how do they make us feel? Which sounds can you use to help you come back to your breathing? Can you think of ways other than sounds that the Buddha inside you might use to call you? Things you see or smell or touch that remind you to come back to your Buddha nature?*

[*A sunset; finding a lost toy; a butterfly; a storm; a flower; dinner cooking; my cat crawling up in my lap; my dog wagging his tail; my favorite stuffed animal.*]

Why do you think the Buddha inside you—your Buddha nature—wants to get your attention?

[*To remind me to be happy; to remind me to love the person I'm with; to remind me to be kind.*]

Wherever you are, it is wonderful to listen for the Buddha, or to look for the Buddha, or to see if you can smell or feel the Buddha calling you.

sharing . . . .

THE MINDFUL SCHOOL BELL
by Ed Glauser, Georgia, USA

I am an elementary school counselor in a conservative town in Georgia that is part of the Bible Belt. I have begun bringing my bell of mindfulness into classrooms and inviting the bell to sound as we mindfully breathe in and out. I saw signs throughout the year that the students and teachers were enjoying the sound of the bell, that it was improving the lives of the school children and teachers, and that it was enriching the community.

I knew I was on the right track when a second grade student told me that she taught her two-year-old brother to breathe mindfully and think of the bell during conflicts at his day-care center. She proudly told me that her brother practiced breathing mindfully when another child bit him on the nose, and her brother chose to think of the bell instead of retaliating. On another occasion, a fourth grader came to my office and told me that he was upset. He just wanted to invite the bell to sound in my office, breathe in and out, and go back to class to resume learning. It worked beautifully for him. He invited the bell three times and said, "Thank you, I feel much better," and went back to class.

In the last weeks before the end of the school year, there were several instances when the bell changed the emotional climate of the school. In the first instance, teachers began asking me to download the bell sound from the website of the Washington Mindfulness Community in Washington, D.C., (mindfulnessdc.org) in order to sound it throughout the school day so students could pause, breathe in and out, and be refreshed.

In the second instance, the bell sound from the computer saved a very heated parent-teacher conference in my office, as each person paused to breathe and to be more mindful of respectfully expressing their displeasure. Last, the school principal, who is also a Southern Baptist preacher, asked me to download the bell on to his computer. He brought the bell to a faculty meeting so all the teachers could breathe together. He also reminded me to remember the bell and breathe when I was in a stressful situation.

It was beautiful to see how the bell of mindfulness and conscious breathing could transform the atmosphere of a public school into a more mindful and respectful environment for everyone, even in a small, Southern Bible Belt town in Georgia. I say, "Amen!"

Pebble Meditation

Breathing in, I see myself as a FLOWER
Breathing out, I feel FRESH

Breathing in, I see myself as a MOUNTAIN
Breathing out, I feel SOLID

Breathing in, I see myself as STILL WATER
Breathing out, I REFLECT things as they are

Breathing in, I see myself as SPACE
Breathing out, I feel FREE

5

i am free: meditation

MANY YEARS AGO, we had a retreat for children in Santa Barbara, California. Many hundreds of children came for the retreat, and their parents came to support them. During that retreat, we invented pebble meditation.

PEBBLE MEDITATION

You may practice pebble meditation at the foot of a tree, in your living room, or wherever you like, but the place should be quiet. You will need a small bell. You can elect one person to lead the pebble meditation session, and whomever you chose should know how to invite the bell to sound.

Each of you can select four pebbles from nature. You can make a little bag in which to keep them. You may like to organize a sitting meditation with your friends or family. If you are with friends, you may invite one or two adults to join you in pebble meditation. Sit in a circle. In the center you may put a flower. After bowing to the flower, sit beautifully in the lotus position (with legs crossed and both feet resting on opposite thighs), or in the half lotus position (with just one foot on the opposite thigh), or in whatever position you like. What is important is that you find a position that is comfortable for you.

Put the four pebbles next to you on your left. Pick up the first pebble, look at it, and then hold it in the palm of your hand. You can rest this hand in the palm of your other hand.

The first pebble represents a flower. *"Breathing in, I see myself as a flower. Breathing out, I feel fresh. Flower, fresh."* Breathe three times, reciting "flower" with each in-breath and "fresh" with each out-breath. You really see yourself as a flower; it's not just imagining. During the time you breathe in, you see yourself as a flower, fresh and lovely. We human beings are a kind of flower in the garden of humanity. Every one of us is a flower. We can be very beautiful, very fresh as a human being. Every one of us has our flowerness that makes us beautiful, fresh, pleasant, lovable. When we have this freshness and beauty, we have a lot to offer to other people and to the world.

When I look at a child, I always see him or her as a flower. Her face is a real flower. His eyes are a flower. Her hand, his tiny foot is a real flower. A child playing is a real flower playing. The flower is beautiful when he is awake, and the flower is also beautiful when she is sleeping. We can see that every child is a real flower, and we wish that they will be a flower for their whole life. Meditation can help preserve our freshness, our flowerness. Many adults have lost their flowerness, their freshness. They have cried and suffered so much. When you are angry, irritated, and mean, you are not fresh at all; you don't look presentable to other people.

One of the ways to restore our freshness is to practice, *"Breathing in, I see myself as a flower."* I don't imagine. I was originally a flower, and the seed of flowerness is still in me. I was born a flower and I want to stay a flower all my life. I am an old person but I try my best to stay fresh. Many children like to come and sit close to me because I know how to restore my freshness, my flowerness. During the four or five seconds of your in- and out-breath, you can do a lot to restore your flowerness—by breathing, smiling, and releasing tension. Smiling is a very easy thing to do. It does not take much time and can release many hundreds of muscles in your face in just one or two seconds. How do you know if your meditation is successful or not? If during the practice you can see yourself as a flower and you feel fresh, then you have succeeded. This is the first practice with the first pebble. When you are finished, place it down on your right.

Now pick up the second pebble. The second pebble represents a mountain. *"Breathing in, I see myself as a mountain. Breathing out, I feel solid. Mountain, Solid."* Say this to yourself as you breathe in and out three times.

Believe it or not, there is a mountain inside each of us. You sit in a very stable position with your back straight and relaxed in a way that makes you feel solid. The best position for practicing this is the lotus position or the half lotus position because you are very firm. Even if someone comes and pushes you or provokes you, you stay solid; you are not carried away by your anger, fear, worry, or despair. You can stay calm, even in the face of provocation and threats. No one can make you afraid anymore. This is very important for your happiness. Solidity makes it possible for us to be happy. Someone who is unstable, someone who is not solid, cannot be a happy person. When you are solid, people can rely on you. When your loved one is solid, you can rely on her. So solidity is something that you can offer to the person you love, like freshness.

The third pebble represents still water. *"Breathing in, I see myself as still water, breathing out, I reflect things as they are. Still water, reflecting."* If you have seen the surface of a lake that is very still, it reflects the mountains, clouds, and trees around it perfectly. You can take a picture of the lake, and it is as if you are taking a picture of the surrounding sky, trees, and mountains.

When you are calm, when you are still, you see things as they truly are. You don't distort things and you are not a victim of wrong perceptions that bring about fear, anger, and despair. When you are not calm, you perceive things incorrectly and you are confused; you misunderstand people and you misunderstand yourself. You make a lot of mistakes and create a lot of suffering for yourself and others. If you are tranquil and peaceful, your perceptions will be more accurate. With the third pebble, I want to cultivate stillness and calm.

Each human being should have enough calm, tranquility, and stillness to be truly happy, so we need the third pebble: still water. Every day we should be able to practice "water, reflecting" to calm our body and mind.

The last pebble represents space and freedom. *"Breathing in, I see myself as space, breathing out, I feel free. Space, free."* Space is freedom, and freedom is the foundation of true happiness. Without freedom, our happiness is not complete. Freedom from what? Freedom from fear, from craving, from anger, from despair, from our projects and worries. The Buddha is someone who is utterly free. That is why his happiness is great. Breathing in, you bring a lot of space into yourself. Breathing out, you bring a lot of space to your beloved ones.

If you love someone, try to offer him more space within and around him and he will be happy. In the art of *ikebana* or flower arranging, you learn that each flower needs space around her to radiate her beauty. Human beings are like this also. Everyone needs some space inside and around us to be truly happy. If we love someone, we should know how to offer him enough space, inside and outside.

If you don't have enough space for yourself, how can you offer space to the person you love? Therefore it's crucial that we know how to cultivate more space for ourselves. If you have freedom and you can offer freedom, you are a true lover. You don't imprison yourself and you don't imprison the person you love. You have freedom in your heart, and you offer freedom to her.

Pebble meditation can help children and adults cultivate more freshness, solidity, stillness, and freedom. It can be done anywhere, with pleasure and without difficulty. I have been doing my best to transmit the most beautiful things I have to my spiritual children and their children.*

---

*You can also share pebble meditation based on the six *paramita*s (generosity, diligence, mindfulness trainings, inclusiveness, meditation, and understanding); or on the Three Jewels (Buddha, Dharma, and Sangha); or on the Four Immeasurable Minds (love, compassion, joy, and inclusiveness). Or, pebbles could represent beloved ones, like mother, father, siblings, grandparents; holding each pebble, we can send our love to that person as we breathe three times.

Exercises for Practicing Pebble Meditation

In addition to the practices below, you can use the guided pebble meditation, Track 5 on the CD.

PEBBLE MEDITATION WITH DRAWING

MATERIALS: bell and inviter, 1 sheet of paper folded in fourths, 4 pebbles for each child, colored felt-tip markers, crayons, pastels, colored pencils, or watercolors

Note: Collect the pebbles yourself or have the children collect them.

TRACK 5

Pebble Meditation

Children are very capable of guiding this meditation for each other, and they often enjoy inviting the bell. Either one child can lead the whole meditation or a different child can guide each one of the four exercises. You may want to offer this practice in one, two, or more sittings depending on your time limits and the energy of the children. You might even take four days to complete the pebble meditation, having the children contemplate just one pebble each day. You can also begin or end each class period or day with five to ten minutes of pebble meditation. You might begin pebble meditation with the song "Breathing In, Breathing Out." What you can say is in *italics*.

TRACK 6

Breathing In, Breathing Out

Let us learn to sing a song that children helped compose to help us practice pebble meditation with a flower, a mountain, still water, and space. It is called "Breathing In, Breathing Out."

Now, let's breathe in and out with the bell, three times.

Wake up the bell, and then invite the bell three times, pausing between each sound.

Take out your four pebbles and put them on your left. Next, open your sheet of paper. You will draw something in each section of your folded paper. In one section, please draw a flower, any kind of flower. As you draw the flower, you can breathe mindfully.

After the children have drawn their flower, say, *A flower represents our fresh-ness. All of us have the capacity to be fresh. If we have lost our freshness, we can practice breathing in and out to restore our freshness. You also are a flower, and you have your flowerness. We are beautiful every time we restore our flowerness.*

With two fingers, pick up one of the pebbles and place it in the palm of your left hand. Look at it with your fresh eyes: The pebble represents a flower. Rest your left hand in your right hand, and begin to practice with the first pebble:

Breathing in, I see myself as a flower.
Breathing out, I feel fresh.
Flower, fresh.

Gently repeat the two key words to yourself as you breathe in and out three times. Each time you recite them, you restore the flowerness in you, and you become fresh. After three breaths, look at your pebble, smile to it, and put it down on your right on the floor beside you.

The second thing I would like you to draw is a mountain. Breathe in and out and smile as you draw the mountain.

After the children have drawn their mountain, say, *A mountain represents solidity and stability. There is a mountain within you, because when you practice sitting and walking, you grow your capacity to be solid and stable. Solidity and stability are very important for our happiness. We know that we have the capacity to be stable, to be solid. If we know how to practice walking mindfully or sitting mindfully, we cultivate our solidity, our stability. That is the mountain within us.*

Now pick up the second pebble and look at it. This pebble represents a mountain. Put it in the palm of your left hand, then rest your left hand in your right and begin to practice with the second pebble:

Breathing in, I see myself as a mountain.
Breathing out, I feel solid.
Mountain, Solid.

Gently repeat the key words as you breathe in and out three times. You have a mountain within. You are capable of being solid and stable. Then put the pebble down to your right.

The third thing I would like you to draw is still water, such as a lake. Breathe in and out and smile as you draw the water.

After the children have drawn still water, say: *Still water reflects the sky, the clouds, and the mountains. Still water is beautiful. When water is still, it reflects things as they are without distorting them. When we learn how to mindfully breathe in and breathe out, we can quiet ourselves. We become calm and serene, no longer the victim of wrong perceptions or illusions. We have the capacity for great clarity, and that is the still water within us. Please pick up the third pebble and look at it. This pebble represents still water. Put it in the palm of your left hand, rest your left hand in your right hand, and begin your practice with the third pebble:*

Breathing in, I see myself as still water.
Breathing out, I reflect things as they truly are.
Water, Reflecting.

Gently repeat this to yourself as you breathe in and out three times. Still water is within you. You are calm, clear, and serene. Then place the pebble to your right.

The fourth thing I would like you to draw is space. You might like to draw the sky, an open field, or a flying bird. Breathe in and out as you draw space.

After the children have drawn space, say, *We need to have space in us to experience freedom and joy. Without space we cannot be happy or peaceful. When we look at a table, we may think it is made of wood. If we look closely, we also see that the table is made of a lot of space. The amount of wood in a table is actually very small. Our body and consciousness are also like this. We may think we are only made of our body, but if we look closely we also see that we are made of our consciousness and many other things. Breathing in and out, we recognize that there is a lot of space within us. When we practice in a way that cultivates space inside of us, we become free and happy.*

Now pick up the fourth pebble. Look at it and smile to it. This pebble represents space. Put it in the palm of your left hand, rest your left hand in your right, and begin the practice with the fourth pebble:

Breathing in, I see myself as space,
Breathing out, I feel free.
Space, free.

Gently repeat this to yourself as you breathe in and out three times. Space is within you. When we cultivate spaciousness inside and outside of us, we can offer this acceptance and generosity to our beloved ones. Like the moon traveling through the beautiful night sky, we have the capacity for space and freedom no matter where we are. Without freedom, no one can be truly happy. When we touch the space inside of us, we are free. Now place the pebble to your right.

After breathing with the four pebbles, you have completed twelve in-breaths and out-breaths. This ends the pebble meditation, but if you enjoy it and want to continue, you may repeat breathing with the four pebbles again. When you are finished, place the pebbles back into your bag, bow to your friends, and breathe as you listen together to one more sound of the bell.

Awaken and invite the bell.

Breathing in and out three times together, let's look at each other and smile, because we have finished a wonderful session of pebble meditation. We bow to each other and stand up.

PEBBLE MEDITATION PRACTICE SHEET

MATERIALS: 1 copy of the practice sheet, pen, pencil, marker or crayon for each child

After children have meditated with their pebbles, invite them to fill out the Pebble Meditation practice sheet, available on the Planting Seeds website. If you would like to make your own practice sheet, ask the children to write the four sets of keywords with a half page of space underneath each one. Have them finish the following sentences to reflect concretely on the meaning of each pebble.

FLOWER   FRESH

I feel fresh, energetic, joyful, and playful when:

_____

[I go swimming; take a shower; wake up from a nap; play with friends; ride my bike]

MOUNTAIN   SOLID

I feel solid, strong, and confident when:

_____

[A friend is sad and I can support him; I do well in a sports activity; I help my younger brother or sister]

WATER   REFLECTING

I feel calm, still, quiet, and focused when:

_____

[I do well in school; I draw or write; I sing; I go for a walk]

SPACE   FREE

I feel free, light, and relaxed when:

_____

[I spend time playing with my friends or parents; I do my favorite activity;
I run down a hill; I play on a swing; I pet an animal]

Underneath each of the sentences and keywords, children can draw a picture of themselves doing this activity.

MAKING PEBBLE MEDITATION BAGS

MATERIALS: yarn, watercolors or fabric paints, markers, ribbons, tapestry needles, children's scissors, buttons, beads, and other decorative items; one 8-inch diameter circle of soft, thin, white or light-colored cloth for each child (For very young children, it is helpful to cut small holes all around the cloth, 1 inch from the edge, with about ½ inch between each hole.)

After the children have learned pebble meditation and collected their four pebbles, invite them to make bags in which to put their pebbles. The children can decorate their cloth circles with the materials you have on hand. If you are using paint or watercolors, allow time for the cloth to dry. When the children have finished decorating the cloth, show them how to thread the yarn through the holes. When they have woven the yarn all the way around, show them how to pull the yarn closed to make a pouch. When you have finished practicing pebble meditation, you can have the children put the pebbles into their new bags until the next time you practice pebble meditation.

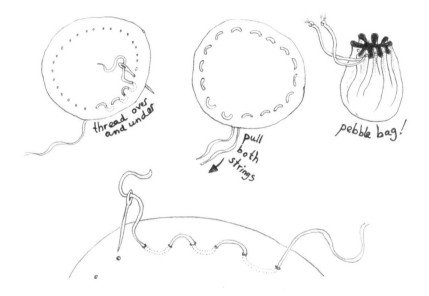

Meditating throughout the Day

GUIDED MEDITATION CARDS

Cut out a copy of the Pebble Meditation cards at the back of the book, download them from the Planting Seeds website, or allow the children to make their own cards. Children might like to take these cards home, share them with family and friends, and practice with them. If you copy the cards in black and white, the children can color them in.

FIVE-FINGER MEDITATION

by Mike Bell, United Kingdom

Start with the index finger of one hand resting on the wrist of the other hand, just below the thumb. Breathing in, slide the finger up the outside of the thumb. Breathing out, slide the finger down the other side of the thumb. Breathing in, slide the finger up the first finger; breathing out, slide the finger down the other side of that finger, and do the same with the remaining three fingers. Or you could simply hold each finger with the other hand for one in- and out-breath. Be aware of the in- and out-breath with the first finger, and then use the four images from pebble meditation for the other four fingers.

SETTING UP A BREATHING ROOM

It would be wonderful if every home had a place to practice pebble meditation. We could call it the Breathing Room or Meditation Room. We may have a room for everything else—a guest room, living room, bedroom, TV room, but we might not have a room for our peace, for our spiritual life, for our nervous system. In every home there should be a Breathing Room. It is a territory of peace, the territory of the Buddha within your own home.

This room is a sacred place. You don't need any furniture, maybe just a few cushions, and perhaps an altar or a table with fresh flowers. If you want, you can have a mini bell to help you in the practice of mindful breathing.

It would be wonderful if every morning the family could practice breathing with one or more pebbles before school and work. This is a powerful way to begin the day. Every time you feel miserable, go to the room, to the territory of the Buddha, and step into the Pure Land. Sit down, listen to the bell, and restore your peace.

Once you are in the meditation room, no one can shout at you any more—you have impunity. And when you hear a member of your family inviting the bell and you know they are practicing to calm down in the Breathing Room, you support them by turning off the TV and not making loud noises. When there is not enough peace in the family, if someone is shouting or very upset, you restore your clarity in the Breathing Room and you know exactly what to do and what not to do. Each person's contribution to the practice of making peace in the family is very important.

A quiet area in a classroom can also be a Breathing Room, a place where students can go if they need to calm down and return to themselves. The space could be in a corner with desks arranged to make a boundary. There could be some chairs there, or a welcoming rug on which to sit or lie.

In many public schools in Germany there are rooms for guided meditation. The children lie on the carpeted floor with lights turned low, and a CD player plays calming music. At Master School near Austin, Texas, there is an outdoor gazebo the children built called the Tranquility Center. Children brought an old chair and ottoman from home and put pillows on the floor. Kids and staff go there to relax, read, nap, or calm down. You can also create a Breathing Room at work.

DEEP RELAXATION FOR YOUNG PEOPLE

Stress and tension are a growing problem for many of us. Even young children are becoming more and more affected by stress as life in our society increasingly speeds up. Deep Relaxation is an opportunity for our body to rest, heal, and be restored. We relax our body, give our attention to each part, and send our love and care to every cell.

If you have trouble sleeping, Deep Relaxation can help. Lying awake on your bed, you may like to practice Deep Relaxation and follow your breathing. This can help you get to sleep. Even if you don't sleep, the practice nourishes you and allows you to rest.

Just as we offer the practice of Deep Relaxation for adults, we have a version for children. It is a practice we can do together as a family in the Breathing Room, or at school with friends or with our class. You can read this text to the children or

> TRACK 7
>
> Deep Relaxation
> for Young People

you can invite several children to take turns reading it for the other children. Older children often enjoy this and can do it very well. Remind them to read slowly and to pause after each sentence. They may even enjoy singing lullabies to the group. You don't have to use the whole practice as offered here; you can focus on fewer parts of the body, or on different parts of the body. Feel free to modify the practice appropriately.

TRACKS 8-12

Relaxing Songs for
Deep Relaxation

Invite the children to lie down or, if this is not possible, to relax in whatever position they are able. Slowly read them the italicized text below. Please skip any parts that are not appropriate for the physical bodies of the children you are working with. After sending care to the parts of the body, sing or play music for the children as they rest. Or you can simply play the relaxing songs for Deep Relaxation on the CD, Tracks 8 through 12. Alternatively, you can play Track 7 on the CD and be guided through the Deep Relaxation. Track 13 is the End of Deep Relaxation.

TRACK 13

End of Deep
Relaxation

Deep Relaxation provides a wonderful chance to allow our bodies to rest. When our body is at ease and relaxed, our mind will also be calm and at peace. The practice of Deep Relaxation is very important for our body and mind to heal. Please take the time to practice it often. You can practice deep relaxation any time of the day—for five or ten minutes when you wake up in the morning, before going to bed in the evening, or during a short break in the middle of a busy day. The most important thing is to enjoy it.

Relax. Close your eyes. Allow your arms to rest gently on either side of your body and let your legs and feet relax and open outward naturally. If your body is not able to do this, please find whatever position is most comfortable for you and relax in whatever position you are able.

Do you know you are a miracle? Your whole body is a miracle, from the hair on the top of your head, all the way down to your littlest toe.

Begin by breathing in and breathing out. When we breathe in, we feel our tummy rise up. When we breathe out, we feel our tummy go down again. Our breathing comes in and out like waves on the ocean, very relaxed, very peaceful. For several breaths, just notice the rise and fall of your belly.

As I breathe in and out, I become aware of my whole body lying down. I feel all the areas of my body that are touching the floor: my heels, the backs of my legs, my bottom, my back, the backs of my hands and arms, the back of my head. With each breath, I feel myself relax deeper and deeper into the floor, letting go of everything, letting go of worries, of fears, of thoughts, and of planning about the future.

Breathing in, I'm aware of my two hands. Breathing out, I completely relax all the muscles in my two hands. Breathing in, I feel lucky to have two good hands. Breathing out, I smile to my two hands. My two hands are so precious! Because of my hands I can play in the sand and build a sand castle. With my two hands I can paint, I can draw, I can write. I can build and fix things, or pet an animal. I can ride a bicycle. I can climb a tree and throw a snowball. I can hold hands with my friend, tie my shoelaces; I can help make cookies, spring rolls, or tamales; I can brush my hair, and much, much more.

Breathing in, I stretch my hands wide. Breathing out, I relax them. My hands are two very good friends, always ready to help me.

Breathing in, I'm aware of my two arms. Breathing out, I allow my arms to completely relax. Breathing in, I feel happy to have two strong arms. Breathing out, I let go of any tight muscles and I feel joy and ease in all the cells of my arms. With my arms I can hug my parents and grandparents. My arms let me play on a swing, go swimming, or throw a football. They help me do a cartwheel, take out the trash, and carry a kitten. Now I have the chance to tell my arms, "thank you!" They do so much for me.

Breathing in, I stretch out my arms. Breathing out, I let my arms rest, completely relaxed. I smile to my two good friends.

Breathing in, I'm aware of my shoulders. Breathing out, I let my shoulders rest and give all their weight to the floor. Breathing in, I send my love to my shoulders. Breathing out, I smile to my shoulders. I am thankful for their strength. Every time I breathe out, I feel them relax more and more.

Breathing in, I'm aware of my two feet. Breathing out, I smile to my feet. I wiggle my toes, all ten of them. How nice to have two feet! With my two feet, I can walk and run, play sports, dance, and ride a bike. My feet love to feel the warm sand when I walk on the beach. When it rains, my feet love to splash in a rain puddle. In the park or playground, my feet love to run and jump and skip. And when I am tired, my two feet love to rest. Thank you, feet!

Breathing in, I stretch my feet and toes. Breathing out, I relax my feet. I feel lucky to have my two feet.

Breathing in, I'm aware of my right leg and my left leg. Breathing out, I enjoy my two legs. My two legs have been growing every day since I was a tiny little baby. They are still growing and changing right now. My growing legs help me stand up straight, each day a little taller. With my two legs, I can sit cross-legged or do the splits. I can play soccer and walk on stilts. Climbing up and down the stairs, walking back and forth to school, I have already walked miles and miles with my own two legs! It feels so good to have my legs.

Breathing in, I stretch out my legs. Breathing out, I let my legs relax. My legs are a miracle and they are always there for me.

Breathing in, I feel my two eyes. Breathing out, I smile to my eyes. Breathing in, I let all the many muscles around my eyes relax. Breathing out, I send my two eyes my love and care. My two eyes are a gift! With my eyes, I can see. I can see you and I can see me. I can see birds flying in the bright blue sky. I can see the yellow moon up above, so high. I can read, write, and watch television. I can watch ants build and I can do long division. When I'm sad, I can cry and let the tears flow. My eyes let everything inside of me show.

Breathing in, I squeeze my eyes shut. Breathing out, I release them and let them relax. Thank you, eyes, for letting me see; there is so much beauty to see around me.

Breathing in, I feel my lungs grow bigger. When I breathe out, I feel them get smaller.

Breathing in, I feel so happy to have two good lungs. Breathing out, I smile to my lungs with kindness. My lungs are so incredible. They help me breathe in and out all day and night, even when I sleep. They bring oxygen into my body and give me the power to speak, to sing, to shout, to whisper, to giggle, and to grumble. When I was just born, the first thing I did was to take a deep in-breath. And ever since then, my lungs have been there for me, every minute of every day.

I breathe the fresh air into my lungs, and breathing out, I let them rest and relax. Thank you lungs for helping me breathe!

Breathing in, I know my heart is beating inside my chest. Breathing out, I enjoy my heart and let it rest. With my in-breath, I send my love to my heart. With my out-breath, I smile to my heart. My heart keeps me alive and it is always there for me, every minute, every day. It never takes a break. My heart has been beating since I was just a four-week-old fetus in my mother's womb. It is a marvelous organ that allows me to do everything I do throughout the day. Breathing in, I know that my heart also loves me. Breathing out, I promise to live in a way that will help my heart to be healthy and strong. With each exhalation, I feel my heart relaxing more and more, and I feel each cell in my heart smiling with ease and joy. (Sing or play music at this time.)

Breathing in, I'm aware of my stomach. Breathing out, I let my stomach relax. As I breathe in, I enjoy my stomach. As I breathe out, I smile to my stomach. I know my stomach works so hard for me. Each day it digests the food I eat and gives me energy and strength. Now I let it rest totally.

As I breathe in, I feel my stomach feeling happy and light. As I breathe out, I feel so thankful for my stomach. It is always there for me.

Now I bring my attention to a place in my body that may be sick or in pain. I take this time to become aware of it and send it my love. Breathing in, I allow this area to rest. Breathing out, I smile to it with kindness. I know that there are other parts of my body that are still strong and healthy. I let these strong parts of my body send their strength and energy to the weak or sick area. I feel the support, energy, and love of the healthy parts of my body penetrating the weak area, soothing and healing it.

As I breathe in, I know my body is a miracle because it can heal when it gets sick. As I breathe out, I let go of any worry or fear I might hold in my body.

Breathing in and out, I smile with love and confidence to the area of my body that is not well.

Breathing in, I feel my whole body lying down. Breathing out, I enjoy the feeling of my whole body lying down, very relaxed and calm. I smile to my whole body as I breathe in and send my love and compassion to my whole body as I breathe out. I feel all the cells in my whole body smiling joyfully with me. I feel gratitude for all the cells in my whole body. I feel the gentle rising and falling of my belly.

Now the practice of Deep Relaxation is over. You can gently move your hands and feet and slowly stretch. Then roll on to one side and sit up. When you are ready, you can open your eyes. Take your time to get up calmly and slowly. Enjoy carrying the peaceful, mindful energy you have generated into the rest of the day.

WATERFALL RELAXATION MEDITATION[*]

You can read the following text slowly to help children learn to relax before meditation.

A beautiful waterfall of white light is flowing down on you. It flows down on your head, helping your head to relax. You feel your head relaxing. The waterfall of light moves down over your neck and shoulders. Your neck and shoulders are relaxing and letting go of all the tension and stress they carry. Now the waterfall flows down over your arms. You feel your arms releasing, there is nothing for your arms to do. The waterfall flows down your back. Your back is letting go and relaxing. The waterfall flows over your chest and stomach, helping your chest and stomach to release. You can feel your chest and stomach relax, letting go of anger, hurt, and sadness. The waterfall moves down over your legs and feet. You feel your legs and feet letting go and resting. The beautiful waterfall of white light is flowing over your

[*]Source: www.buddhanet.net

whole body. You are very peaceful and rested. Just stay in the waterfall of light for a few moments, and feel how it relaxes and heals your body.

Child's Question and Answer

During every retreat, Thay offers a Question and Answer session in which anyone can come up on the stage and ask him a question. Children and teens always go first. Here is a question from one of these sessions:

CHILD'S QUESTION: *Dear Thay, how many hours of meditation do you practice daily, and how many hours of that are sitting meditation and how many are walking meditation?*

THAY: Every time I sit, it is sitting meditation. Whether I am sitting in the lotus position, the half-lotus position, or the chrysanthemum position, that is sitting meditation. I am not a good mathematician, so I don't count very well. My practice is to do this: any time I sit down, it is sitting meditation. I want to sit quietly and peacefully. During the Dharma talk, although I have to speak, that is also sitting meditation. I sit with stability, with peace. You don't only count the time sitting in the meditation hall, you count the time sitting everywhere. Sitting in the grass, sitting on a hill—any sitting is sitting meditation.

Anytime you move your feet and touch the ground, anytime you go from one place to another, you can practice walking meditation. In Plum Village it is recommended that we do that. We don't do it just for one hour or one and a half hours a day, but all day long. Every time you walk it should be walking meditation, because it brings you more happiness and more peace than walking in forgetfulness. Also, we're not supposed to talk while we walk because we have to invest ourselves completely in the walking. With every step you give 100 percent of yourself so that you can produce the energy of stability and peace. If you talk, you don't have as much energy for walking. If you need to listen to someone, you stop and listen with 100 percent of yourself.

The practice in Plum Village is not to just have some time in the day for practicing. You try to practice the whole day. Whether you are cooking or washing, you follow your breath. If you do things mindfully, that is already meditation. In Plum Village we practice continuous meditation and we want to do everything in a relaxed way. Driving a car, talking on the telephone, washing our dishes—we want to do everything peacefully. We consider each thing to be as important as the time of sitting meditation. Every activity is for us to enjoy.

SLOW WALKING*

Gather the group into a circle. *Let's do something to make ourselves more aware of how our beautiful bodies work. Form a line and begin moving in a circle around the room. Just move as you normally do, but pay attention to the movements of your body.* Walk around the circle a few times.

Slow down so that it takes you two or three minutes to move around the room. Feel how your feet make contact with the ground, feel the swing of your arms, feel how everything fits together.

Now move as slowly as your body can. Take a very long time just to take one step. Be aware of every muscle your body has to move in order to take a step. Do this for three or four minutes. *Now stop where you are, relax, and take a few breaths.*

WALKING MINDFULLY**

The following suggestions will help children become aware of how their bodies move in different situations, and also of how their bodies can convey their feelings.

---

*Reprinted with the permission of Simon & Schuster, Inc., from *The Centering Book: Awareness Activities for Children, Parents, and Teachers* by Gay Hendricks and Russel Wills. Copyright © 1975 by Prentice-Hall, Inc. All rights reserved.

**Source: Fiona Clarke and assorted drama games books

Imagine walking in snow, leaving deep footprints. Imagine walking on thin ice, being very careful not to break the ice. Imagine each time you put your foot down and lift it up a beautiful lotus springs up from the ground, so you are leaving a trail of lotuses wherever you go.

STUDENTS COMMENT ON WALKING MEDITATION

"I learned how to let go of pressure."

"I want to do slow walking before exams."

"When I walk I want to try to reduce my speed and relax so I can be aware of the surroundings."

Walk like a busy businessperson; like a hairy beast; like a balloon; like a soldier; a burglar; a robot. Imagine you are wearing a crown or a cape. Imagine carrying a bucket of water on your head. Imagine you are rushing. See how your movements change.

Imagine walking through a beautiful place, feeling very relaxed and happy. Imagine walking through a very dark alley, hearing noises, and feeling scared. Imagine you have been away from your family for a week; how would you greet them when you see them again?

Walk in large strides, in tiny steps. Walk through snow; through a raging river; across stepping stones; through the surf; through hot sand in the desert; on a tightrope; like a cat; on a rope bridge; with metal legs; like a baby; on hot coals; like an ice-skater; like a shy person; like a confident person; like an elephant; like an old person. Now walk slowly, becoming aware of as many details of your walking as possible. Notice how the heel of your foot, then the ball of your foot touches the floor. Lift and move your other foot slowly. See if you can feel how you keep your balance. Let your body relax in each step, and put all of your weight on the foot you're standing on. Breathe deeply. Now breathe in whenever you lift your foot and breathe out whenever you place it down. Continue to walk in this way for another minute.

TRACK 14

Walking Meditation

You can play the song "Walking Meditation" for the children and teach it to them.

SENDING WISHES AT THE START AND END OF EACH DAY

MATERIALS: bell, inviter, candle, incense, and matches
(If the room is not well ventilated or if someone is allergic, you can offer a flower or a pebble.)

The way in which the class or group gathers at the beginning of the day and at the end of a day can be very beneficial for the whole group of children as well as the adults taking care of them. We have a fresh opportunity to start the day in the best possible way and to return to a more peaceful state of being at the end of a day. We can help the children to develop a habit of being more reflective, to return to a space within them that radiates warmth and light.

Invite a sound of the bell. You can adapt the following meditation to begin or end the day:

Allow yourself to settle into your seat and bring all of yourself into this moment. In the quiet of this moment, feel where inside of you there is the most warmth and love and space. It could be where your heart is; if so, put a hand or both hands on your heart. It could be up in your mind; if so, gently hold your head with a hand or both hands. It could be elsewhere in your body, so put your hand or both hands on that place. Really focus on that place where you feel love, warmth, and spaciousness.

From within this space, feel the wish or wishes that naturally arise and voice themselves. What is this wish? Is it a wish for someone you love? Is it a wish for more than one person? Is it a wish for someone you don't like? Is it a wish for yourself? Is it a wish for other forms of life, such as animals, plants, or minerals?

At this point, ask if any child would like to share their wish with the group. A child may want to wish for peace in the world, the happiness of their parents, or to get along with their sister or brother. Now ask for a volunteer to light a candle, which represents sending the wishes out in light and warmth, and another to light an incense stick, which represents the fragrance and beauty of the wishes.

> TRACK 15
>
> ....
>
> May the Day
> Be Well

Invite a sound of the bell when the incense has been offered so that the whole group can send and release their wishes in the form of light, warmth, and fragrance. End by singing together "May the Day Be Well."

sharing. . . . .

HOW MEDITATION HELPS ME

An Interview with Chiara (age 9) and Siena (age 11) by Sister Jewel, European Institute of Applied Buddhism, Germany

How would you explain the practice of mindfulness?

CHIARA: The practice is sort of like relaxing, but it's a way to feel the way you're breathing. Like when you pray to God, you are, like, meditating to the Buddha; you are praying to the Buddha by listening to your breath. It's like listening to our own breath when we hear the bell. We stop because it's the Buddha saying, "Stop and listen to your breath." That's how I share with my friends.

I feel more relaxed when I stop for the bell, but sometimes I can't always stop. Like when we hear the recess bell at school, we have to go into the school. So sometimes I listen to the bell while I'm running. I listen to my breathing a lot, even when there is no bell. I like to listen to my breathing because it helps me to slow down and stuff. It can also tell you if you're scared and you need to stop.

Do you meditate?

CHIARA: I try to meditate when I'm not tired. I try to be awake when I meditate. Sometimes it's good just to breathe and not think about all these things. But sometimes I can't sit still, so I think about things—like what I should do for New Year's Eve, and should I say such-and-such to my friend?

When I meditate, I'm always refreshing my breath. I'm meditating every second. When listening to the teacher, I'm still. I'm not moving all over the place. When I do a math problem, I take time off to breathe because my mind is too full, and then I check over my work. You just need to slow some things down. Sometimes people say, "Hurry up, we have to get something done," but it's better to breathe because then you can think more.

Do you think mindfulness makes you smarter?

CHIARA: Mindfulness makes you wiser, because you have all that time to think things over.

Do you and your sister get along better after learning about the practice?

CHIARA: She and I get along better now, but sometimes I just get really angry. I have a high temper—I get angry easily. That's why I like to breathe and stop, because I feel so sorry for the people I always yell at. I don't mean to, but I can't help it. If something doesn't go my way, I get mad and *then* I think it over. But now I try to think it over *before* I get mad.

How?

CHIARA: I sort of think about why I'm mad, because sometimes I have a really bad temper over nothing. So I ask, "Why am I getting mad? This is a silly thing to be upset over." That helps me calm down.

Sometimes I feel I need to scream over nothing. That's not what I want. It's not good for me. My mom tries to help; she laughs and makes me laugh. She says, "Make that face again; I want to see that face!" She helps me out.

How would you explain mindfulness practice or meditation?

SIENA: In cartoons, people levitate and stuff, but that's not really what meditation is. It's going inside yourself and being with yourself and realizing what your body needs. Or it's different kinds of practices—like praying for someone else, like for them to get well.

Have you helped your friends with the practice?

SIENA: Yeah, probably. One thing I notice is that kids get more moody as they get older. One time my friend got really mad at another friend. To help her when she gets mad, sometimes I take a walk with her around the basketball court. We don't say much; we just walk. I don't know what she's thinking about—probably the person she's mad at, but I look down at my feet and think about both her and the other person she's mad at. I send them prayers to help both of them feel better. Sometimes I just leave her alone because it's nice to be by yourself for a while.

She usually feels better after this. She apologizes or she hangs out with all of us again. You can tell she's apologizing even if she doesn't say it in words.

How do you practice with your sister?

SIENA: When we fight, we both go to our own beds. She organizes her room while I sit and read. We'll back away from each other and breathe. Or she'll go out and have breakfast. I follow my breathing for three breaths and then do something else, or I try to apologize. I think she stays with her breathing, too. At least she notices it, but I don't know for sure because I'm on the other side of the room.

6

strengthening connections to each other and the earth

IF YOU PLANT A SEED OF CORN and tend it, within a couple of weeks it will sprout and grow. Now imagine you knelt down and talked to this young plant and asked, "My dear young plant of corn, do you remember the time you were a seed of corn?" If it could talk, the plant of corn might say, "Me, a seed of corn? I don't believe it!" The plant of corn may have completely forgotten that she was once a seed. So you tell her, "Dear young plant of corn, I know. It was I who planted you in this pot. I'm sure that you were a grain of corn. I watered you every day, and one day you sprouted and sent forth your first leaves." Suppose you described to the young stalk what has happened to her, perhaps then she would remember where she came from.

We are like that corn plant. The moment when our mother conceived us, you and I, we were very small, much smaller than a seed of corn, but also a tiny seed. That seed contained both our father and our mother in it. We are the continuation of our father and mother, but not many of us remember that. After conception that seed multiplied very quickly. During the first hour after conception, it multiplied into one thousand cells. And we continued to slowly grow this way.

In the womb of our mother, most of us had a good time. The weather there was perfect! We were in a very soft place, surrounded by water, and we floated in it, very comfortable. Our mother breathed for us, ate for us, and smiled for us. We didn't have to do anything, we could just enjoy. In Vietnam we have a very beautiful expression to describe our mother's womb: the palace of the child. We stayed there about nine months. We didn't have to worry about anything at all. There was no worry, no fear, no desire—that's paradise.

But when we were born, the situation changed completely. We had been attached to our mother by the umbilical cord, through which oxygen and food nourished us. When we were born, the umbilical cord was cut, and we were on our own. It was a very difficult moment and a dangerous moment also, because our mother could no longer breathe for us. We had to breathe on our own. It was so difficult because there was liquid in our lungs. We had to push it out in order to take our first in-breath. When we could do that, we knew that we would survive. We had been afraid that we would not survive. It was the first time we experienced fear.

Once outside of our mother, we could not do anything for ourselves. Someone had to take care of us. We weren't capable of doing anything. We had arms and feet, but we didn't know how to use them. We had to rely on our mother or our father. And we began to feel fear. Along with that original fear was the desire to survive, the original desire. As we grow up we have other desires, but every desire in us is just a continuation of that original desire, the desire to survive.

We may behave like the plant of corn. We may not remember we were once in the womb of our mother. We are surprised to learn that we have been a tiny seed. We may not have completely forgotten, but we have almost forgotten that there was a period of time when we were so comfortable in the palace of the child, in that paradise. If from time to time you feel some kind of nostalgia for paradise, you know that you have not completely forgotten the paradise in which you spent nine months.

There's one thing that we should remember. We begin as a very tiny seed, and in that seed there is the presence of our father and our mother and all our ancestors. It's like the plant of corn that is a continuation of the seed of corn.

We are the continuation of our fathers and mothers. That is a fact. If we recognize the fact that the plant of corn is the continuation of the seed of corn, then we have to also accept the truth that we are the continuation of our parents or caretakers, whether or not they are our biological parents. Maybe it will be helpful to go to your father and look at him, and say something like this: "Daddy, do you know that I am your continuation?" In fact, when you are a continuation of something or someone, you are not a completely different entity than that someone. The young plant of corn can't say, "I don't know the seed of corn. I'm something completely different from the seed of corn." That's not the truth because the corn plant has come from the seed of corn. She is *one* with the seed of corn. She doesn't look like a seed of corn, but nevertheless, she is a continuation of the seed of corn.

When a little girl gets angry with her father, what happens? She is actually getting angry at herself, because she is a continuation of her father. When we practice meditation, we realize that our father is inside of us and is present in every cell of our body. Breathing in, I say hello to my father in every cell of my body. Breathing out, I smile to my mother in every cell of my body. In fact, every cell of my body contains the presence of my mother, my father, and my ancestors. I am just a continuation. When I get angry with my mother, it's somehow like I get angry with myself. We cannot say that you and your mother are two different people. But we also cannot say that you two are the same person. You are not exactly the same person as your father. But you are not entirely another person either. It's called "no sameness, no otherness" or "neither the same nor different." That's the teaching of the Buddha.

When we look at the family album and see ourselves as a five-year-old child, we ask ourselves, "Am I the same person as the child in the album?" Now we are thirty or forty, and we look so different from the little boy or girl in the album. That we are the same person is difficult to believe, but in fact we are the continuation of that little boy or girl. Our body is different now, our feelings, our perceptions are different now, but we come from that little boy or girl. When someone asks if you are the same person as that little boy or girl, you can say, "Well, it doesn't seem that I'm exactly the same, because I look and feel different now. But I'm not an entirely different person either, because I come from him or from her, I am their continuation." That is what the Buddha means by the Middle Way—that we are neither the same person, nor are we a totally different person. This is the teaching of no sameness, no otherness. We should take the time to talk to our fathers and mothers about that. The fact is that when you get angry at your father, you somehow get angry at yourself. There's no way to remove our fathers and our mothers from ourselves. That is why we practice to reconcile with them in us.

There was a young man who got so angry at his father, he declared, "That man, I don't want to have anything to do with him!" But he can't remove his father from himself, there's no way; he's a continuation of his father. My mother is myself; that's the truth. My father is also myself. I don't have a completely different self from my mother, my father. It is the Buddha who reminds us of this. So every time you have difficulty with your fathers and your mothers, think again. Look deeply and try to solve the problem in the light of the Buddha's teaching. "No sameness, no otherness" is a very deep teaching of the Buddha.

> TRACK 16
>
> Watering Seeds
> of Joy

You may like to hear and learn the song, "Watering Seeds of Joy," which helps us to see we are a continuation of our parents and our ancestors. It is a chant that I wrote and my students have put it to music. The chant begins with the words,

My mother, my father, they are in me,
and when I look, I see myself in them.

Nurturing Compassion and Community

BEGINNING ANEW CEREMONY FOR FAMILIES

MATERIALS: bell and inviter, vase of flowers

We prepare for this practice at retreats by inviting the children to make cards for their caregivers the day before the ceremony. They write down all the things they appreciate and love about them and decorate the cards. They will offer their cards during the Beginning Anew ceremony. Also we tell the adults beforehand that they should come prepared by bringing with them objects from nature that represent the beautiful qualities that they appreciate in their child.

This beautiful practice allows adults and children to appreciate each other. One little four-year-old boy thanked his mom for always washing all the dirty dishes at home. One grown-up knelt reverently in front of her children as she proceeded to appreciate each of them. It can be a very joyful and moving session for everyone who attends.

If there is time, have the children make a special treat for the adults to serve at the beginning of the ceremony. If there isn't time for this, a tray of cookies can be attractively arranged and served. Begin the ceremony by quietly passing the tray around and enjoying the cookies for a few minutes in silence.

The setup is similar to the adults' practice of Beginning Anew (see Chapter Three). We sit in a circle; most of the children choose to sit near their adults. A vase of flowers or a simple arrangement is placed in the center of the circle. Because the children also go up to get the flowers, it's best to keep the arrangement small and easy for them to hold.

We can begin with a song. When everyone is seated, one of the children can invite three sounds of the bell before we offer a short but complete introduction to the practice of Beginning Anew.

Points to mention:

- The main practices of Beginning Anew are to express our appreciation for our loved ones and also to apologize for any mistakes we have made. When we don't do either of these often enough, our relationships become stagnant. Communication becomes difficult as hurts accumulate, and we don't feel fresh or happy when our beauty, our talents and skills are not appreciated and nourished. We need to do this regularly; once a week is good. Friday evening may be a good time so that then we can enjoy the weekend together.

- We call expressing our appreciation "watering the flower" in the other person, because we each have a flower in us—our freshness, humor, joy, and lightheartedness. We need to help water and maintain the freshness of the flower in our beloved ones. Often we only speak out when something is wrong, but so many good things are happening all the time that we forget to notice. Our child may be in good health, our partner may be helping out with some household chores. We should not just complain when things go wrong, but take time to name all that we are grateful for. When our flower is watered regularly, it is much easier for us to accept constructive criticism and cheerfully change our behavior to be more supportive of the family.

- Share how the practice can help us nourish a positive and optimistic outlook on our loved ones. When one person's flower is watered, we all feel our flower is watered.

- When the introduction is finished, the facilitator can practice flower watering first as an example for everyone.

Invite the children to read what they have written in the cards to their adults if they want to; otherwise, they can simply offer it to them. Once all the children have shared, adults can present their object from nature to their children, expressing how it represents their good qualities.

If there is time, you can do another round and invite the adults to share what they can do to bring more happiness to their family. This is a positive way of sharing your regrets and your determination to do better. Some adults have shared that they want to work less so they can spend more time with their children, or that they want to be more patient and take better care of themselves so they can avoid getting irritated and reacting out of anger. Some share that they want to affirm their children more and give them more space to be who they are. Then the children can share; they often share really lovely and concrete resolutions. Some have shared that they will make more of an effort to listen when asked to do something and not make their adults ask ten times before they do it; others express regret that they have not been as kind as they would like to be with their siblings and that they want to share more and fight less.

If participants are comfortable with it, it is wonderful to end Beginning Anew with the practice of hugging meditation between friends and family members.

HUGGING MEDITATION

Stand facing a family member. Look into his or her eyes. (If the adults are too tall, they can kneel down.) Join your palms and bow to each other. Hug slowly and gently. Take three breaths in each other's arms. With the first breath, we are aware that we are still alive. With the second breath, we are aware that the other is still alive. With the third breath, we feel happy and grateful to hold them in our arms. Look at each other. Join your palms and offer each other a final bow.

WATERING FLOWERS

MATERIALS: colored pens, pencils, or markers; and for each child a large drawing of a flower head with a circle in the center, with as many petals as there are people in the circle

Sitting in a circle, each child can write his own name in the center of the flower. Then he can write a quality or something that he likes about himself in one of the petals. If some children can't write much, encourage them to draw something in the petal or an adult can transcribe their words.

Everyone passes their picture to the person on their left. Then everyone fills in the next petal and writes a good quality of the person whose name is in the center. At the end of the session everyone should have a flower full of good qualities about themselves offered by each person in the group. You can do the same thing with rays of the sun showing a child's strengths. Each child draws a picture of the sun with large sunrays. Put a photo of the child in the center or have them draw their own face there. The compliments they received in flower watering can be written in short form in the rays themselves.

You can also do this exercise without the drawing and just give the children the chance to have their flower watered by every other child in the circle. They can give compliments, thanks, or notice positive qualities in the child. There is a fifth-grade teacher in Germany who hands out a sheet of paper to each student in the class with the names of every student (and herself, too!) down the left-hand column of the page. Every student writes one sentence appreciating every other person in the class. Then, she takes these sheets, cuts them carefully, and pastes all the positive qualities about one student on a single page to copy and hand to them. It is time-consuming but she notices that the atmosphere changes dramatically in her classroom after this, becoming much warmer and more open.

You may like to end a session of flower watering or Beginning Anew by singing together the song "Dear Friends."

> Visit the Planting Seeds website to learn this song

TOUCHING OUR BUDDHA NATURE

We know that a Buddha lives inside of each of us. It's not the man who lived a long time ago, of course, but the nature of that man. Buddha nature lives inside each of us. What do you think Buddha nature is like?

[Happy, generous, compassionate, kind, loving, open, free, patient, etc.]

If children need help coming up with wholesome characteristics, you might suggest this: *Think of someone you love very much. Do you sometimes see the Buddha nature in that person? What does that person do? How does that person show you her Buddha nature?*

It is usually easy to see the Buddha nature in someone we love. But Buddha nature is in everyone, even people we don't think we like at all. Think of someone you don't like very much. Have you ever seen the Buddha nature peek out of that person even a little bit?

What did it look like?

[The person smiled; the person once said something nice to a friend of mine; the person likes my cat.]

Why is it important for us to remember to look for the Buddha nature in ourselves and in everyone we meet?

[So that we can love ourselves and others; so we can be happy and make others happy; so we can all have peace.]

Let's learn a song about how we feel when we notice our friend's Buddha nature. Sing:

Dear friends, dear friends, let me tell you how I feel.
You have given me such treasure, I love you so.

What do you think the treasure is that we sing about in this song? Could it be our friend's Buddha nature? How do we feel about our friends when they show us their Buddha nature?

[*We love her; we feel happy; we feel grateful.*]

What things can help our Buddha nature grow stronger and more beautiful? When you sit and breathe mindfully, when you walk mindfully and eat mindfully, do you feel your Buddha nature is more alive? Let's sing the song again.

Note: After the children have learned the words, it is fun to sing the song as a round in two or three parts.

This song is a good way to say thank you to your friend or to someone in your family. When might you want to sing this song?

[*When my brother doesn't hit me; when my mom gives me a surprise in my lunch box; when daddy reads me a story; when my grandmother makes up a song for me; when my friend lets me play with his rollerblades.*]

BOWING

MATERIALS: colored felt-tipped pens

Bowing is a deep form of communication. A bow may mean hello, thank you, good-bye, or excuse me. But it's not just a way to be polite. It's a way of recognizing and honoring the Buddha or the awakened nature in each of us. We bring our palms together carefully to form a beautiful lotus flower at the level of our heart. Then we look at the eyes of the person we will bow to and we smile. We say silently, "A lotus for you," as we breathe in and, "A Buddha to be!" as we breathe out and bow from our waist. Then we straighten up, look at the eyes of the other person, and smile. Isn't that an easy gift to give someone? Please practice with a friend.

Allow each child time to bow to a friend.

Instead of a lotus, you might want to give something else to a friend or to someone in your family. Maybe you will put your hands together, look in the eyes of your friend, and say to yourself, "An apple for you, a Buddha to be!" or "A sunny day for you, a Buddha to be!" or "A smile for you, a Buddha to be!" and then bow.

Give enough time for each child to practice bowing with another child and with you, "giving" whatever gift they choose to give.

How does it make you feel to bow to the Buddha in someone?

[Happy, like I'm watering the seeds of my friend's happiness.]

How does it make you feel when someone bows to you?

[Happy, grateful, loved.]

When you can, please practice bowing with the people in your family too.

Invite children to draw simple faces on each other's thumbs, using the colored pens. The "thumb people" can practice bowing respectfully. The thumb people might also have conversations with each other or sing to each other.

THE SECOND BODY SYSTEM[*]

We speak to the children about how we have our own body, but now, with the second body system, we will also have a second body. We will care for someone else in our group in the same way as we care for ourselves. We will look after our second body with concern and kindness. If we go out to play or go to a school event, we want to make sure our second body is there and doesn't get left behind. Before going anywhere as a class, the teacher can call for a "second body check"—when the students check for their second body. If the second body isn't there, the student should let the teacher know where he is (maybe in the bathroom, or sick, etc.). In this way, each child becomes used to taking responsibility for another child and also to being cared for by someone else.

If our second body is sad, sick, or having trouble, we try to help or ask someone else to help her. If our second body has missed class, we try to help her

[*] To read a similar practice, *The Secret Friend*, see www.plantingseedsbook.org

catch up on what she missed. We can also just do little things from time to time to make our second body happy, like sharing something nice with her, expressing our appreciation, or including her in our games. This can help to make the classroom environment more like a family.

We take care of someone, but a third person is also taking care of us. We have a second body, but we are also the second body of someone else. We make a chain so everyone is cared for. If your second body is sick or absent for a while, you are then responsible for his second body too, so that no one is forgotten. (If you like, you could also call it the practice of the Guardian Angel. All of the children have someone to protect and are also protected by their own Guardian Angel.) This practice has on many occasions helped us avoid leaving someone on an outing. When the children really practice it, it can be quite a powerful lesson in interconnection.

After explaining how the second body system works, ask one child to begin and choose another student to be her second body. Encourage her to choose someone she may not know so well, but who also will not be too difficult for her to take care of (it may be someone who sits near her in class). Then, the second person chooses a third person, and the third person chooses a fourth, until the last student in the class finally chooses the student who picked first. If the choosing will create some hurt feelings, then there are more random ways to assign second bodies. Pick names from a hat. Or, ask the group to form a circle without giving any instructions first. Each person can take care of the person standing to their right. Ask a student to make a drawing or artwork of the second body chain and post it up in the classroom so the students can remember who their second body is.

If it is appropriate for the children in your group, you can form a circle and invite everyone to massage the shoulders of their second body while simultaneously receiving a massage from their guardian angel or protector. This is a wonderful way to gather energy and create connection before going on an outing together. Students should be instructed to massage the other person gently, with mindfulness and respect.

MANTRAS OF LOVE

You can read or summarize this teaching for the children: *When we love someone, we want to give her things. We can make him a cake or offer him flowers. If we are too busy, we may give her money. But the best thing, the best kind of gift that we can offer the people we love is our freshness. If you practice to breathe in and become a flower and breathe out to feel fresh, then you are yourself; that is the most wonderful kind of gift.*

Suppose you tell your mom, "I have a gift for you." Your mom may ask you, "Where is the gift?" Then you point to yourself and say, "I am the gift!" You are fresh like a flower. You are solid like a mountain. You are calm, peaceful, like still water. You are free like space. That is what you want to offer to the person you love. If you do not have any freshness, solidity, peace, or freedom, you don't have much to offer to the person you love. To have freshness, solidity, peace, freedom, you have to practice the Dharma. You cannot buy these things in a supermarket. So if you are a lover, you know that the best kind of gift you can make to your beloved one is your presence, that is fresh, solid, calm, and free. To love means to be there for him or for her. How can you love if you are not there?

It takes only three seconds, as you breathe in, to bring your mind back to your body in order to be truly there for your beloved. You breathe in mindfully, you become fresh and calm, and you go to him and say this mantra, "Mommy, daddy, I am here for you." Your presence is peaceful, fresh, and that is why you can offer a lot of happiness. "My gift to you is my presence. I have some freshness, some solidity, some peace, and some freedom to offer you."

"I am here for you," *is the first mantra. You can practice it in your own language, you don't have to recite it in Pali, Sanskrit, or Tibetan. It's perfectly alright for those in other spiritual traditions to practice the first mantra. It is the practice of mindfulness, which helps you become present in the here and now, available to offer your presence to your beloved.*

If your beloved one is not with you, you can send an email or use the telephone to practice the first mantra. Call your dad at the office and say, "Daddy, do you know something? I am here for you." There is happiness, love, and calm in your voice, and that will make him very happy. You may like to practice this mantra today, perhaps several times.

The second mantra is to recognize that your beloved is very precious to you. You breathe mindfully and when you have become fully present, you go to her, look into her eyes and recite the second mantra: "Darling, I know you are there, alive, for me, and I'm so happy." *You can say this to your mom or dad or anyone you love very much. Imagine what it would be like for you if your mom or dad were no longer there. You would suffer a lot. So the second mantra helps you appreciate the presence of the people you love. If your beloved one ignores you or is not aware that you are there, you don't feel loved. If your beloved is mindful and knows that you are there, you feel very happy. When you practice the first and second mantras with your adults, right away they feel happy and you feel happy. Do your best to practice the second mantra today.*

You will need the third mantra when your beloved one is not feeling well, is suffering, or upset. Fresh like a flower, peaceful like still water, you go to him and you recite the third mantra, "Darling, I know you suffer, that is why I am here for you." *When you practice this mantra, the other person suffers less right away. Even before you do anything to help him, he suffers less because you are there for him. He no longer feels alone. You can practice the first two mantras every day, and practice the third mantra whenever you see that your beloved suffers.*

THE THREE MANTRAS CALLIGRAPHY

MATERIALS: paper, markers, crayons or watercolors, and calligraphy brushes with ink, if the children are going to make calligraphies of the mantras

Write the three mantras on the board or a large sheet of paper that all the children can see. Begin by inviting the children to discuss the three mantras. *When might you use one of these mantras, and with whom? Has anyone said something like this to you before? How did it make you feel?* Invite pairs of children to come up and demonstrate each of the mantras.

If you have copies of calligraphies by Thay or other artists, show the children a few examples of different styles of this artistic writing. Ask, *What do you feel when you look at the calligraphies? Why do you think the words are written in this style? What do you think the artist is trying to communicate?*

Discuss the tradition of calligraphy in many Asian cultures and the importance of hanging up words of wisdom in our surroundings to help us remember to be mindful and touch the seeds of awakening in us. If possible, invite someone skilled in calligraphy to demonstrate some simple techniques for writing calligraphy as a mindfulness practice.

Invite the children to write the three mantras beautifully on a sheet of paper, or one mantra per sheet of paper. They can experiment with different calligraphy styles. Encourage the children to put them up at home so they will remember to practice them. Post copies of each calligraphy around the room.

TOUCHING THE EARTH FOR YOUNG PEOPLE

MATERIALS: bell and inviter

Touching the Earth is a practice developed by Thich Nhat Hanh to help us connect with the many different aspects of who we are: our blood and spiritual families; the country we live in; and all beings: animals, plants, and minerals. This is a

TRACK 17
....
Touching the Earth
for Young People

version for young people written by Sister Steadiness and Sister Swiftness.* If you have an altar or sacred place in the room, invite the children to touch the

---

* For the original text for adults, see *Teachings on Love*, by Thich Nhat Hanh (Berkeley, CA: Parallax Press, 1998, 2007).

earth with their heads pointing in that direction. It is also very powerful to do the practice outside directly on the earth. You can read the text below or use the guided practice on the CD, Track 17.

INTRODUCTION: *Touching the Earth helps us in many ways. It can help you touch your nature of connectedness, your "no sameness and no otherness," with your adults, friends, and all beings. When you feel restless or lack confidence in yourself, or when you feel angry or unhappy, you can kneel down and touch the Earth deeply. Touch the Earth as if it were your favorite thing or your best friend.*

The Earth has been there for a long time. She is mother to all of us and she knows everything. Just before his enlightenment, the Buddha experienced some doubt and fear, so he asked the Earth to be his witness—to witness his awakening. The Earth appeared to him as a beautiful mother. In her arms she carried flowers and fruit, birds and butterflies, and many different animals, and she offered them to the Buddha. The Buddha's doubts and fears instantly disappeared.

Whenever you feel unhappy, come to the Earth and ask for her help. Touch her deeply, the way the Buddha did. Suddenly, you too will see the Earth with all her flowers and fruit, trees and birds, animals, and all her other living beings. All these things she offers to you.

> TRACK 18
> ....
> Gatha for
> Planting a Tree

You have more opportunities to be happy than you ever thought. The Earth shows her love to you and her patience. She sees you suffer, she helps you, and she protects you. When you die, she takes you back into her arms. With the Earth you are very safe. She is always there, in all her wonderful expressions of trees, flowers, butterflies, and sunshine. Whenever you are tired or unhappy, the practice of Touching the Earth can heal you and restore your joy.

The gatha for planting a tree can help us take refuge in the earth. You can play and teach the song "Gatha for Planting a Tree."

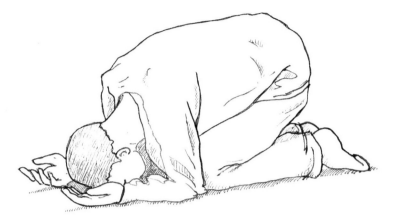

When we touch the earth, we breathe in and, joining our palms, touch them to our forehead and then our heart. This is to unify our mind and body. Breathing out, we open our palms and bend down, either kneeling and touching our forehead to the floor (the child's pose in yoga), or laying our whole body flat on our belly and turning our head to one side. We turn our palms upward, in a gesture of openness, receptiveness, and surrender. We relax completely and allow the words to enter deeply our body and mind. We listen to three sounds of the bell.

Wake up the bell and invite it three times, pausing between each sound. Then stop the bell audibly.

Touching the earth, I see that I am a child of the earth.

Invite the bell one time; children touch the earth.

The earth is like my mother or father. From the earth I receive delicious foods to eat— wheat to make bread, rice, beans, apples, carrots, and even chocolate from cocoa beans. The earth gives us cotton and wool to make our clothes, and wood and stone to make our homes. The earth takes such good care of me. I feel happy to live on the earth.

I feel my body lying on the earth. I feel my arms and my legs and my face touching the ground. I feel that the earth is solid and can support me. I see the earth covered with many plants, trees, and beautiful flowers, making the air clean and pure. As I breathe in I can feel the fresh, cool air fill my body. I feel calm and relaxed. I feel happy and safe on the earth.

Invite the bell one time; children stand up.

★★★

Touching the earth, I feel connected to my parents.

Invite the bell one time; children touch the earth.

I am the child of my parents, even though I may not live with both of them now. I see my parents and I smile to them. I want both my parents to be happy. I want them to be safe and free from all worries.

Sometimes adults get angry with me and I feel hurt. Sometimes they're so busy they don't seem to have time for me, and I feel sad. But other times they take care of me and we can laugh and play together and have fun. My family has taught me so many things, like how to read, or sing, or do math, or make cookies. I feel thankful to them. I know that my parents were children too, and they felt sad and hurt sometimes, just like me. I know they have had many difficulties in their lives, and I don't feel angry with them.

I think of my parents, I feel their love and support, and I feel happy. I know my parents need my freshness and my smiles to make them happy too.

Invite the bell one time; children stand up.

★★★

Touching the earth, I am happy to be me.

Invite the bell one time; children touch the earth.

I am a young girl or boy living on the planet Earth. Sometimes I feel small like a tiny bug or a spider happily crawling in the grass. Sometimes I feel big, like a huge, old tree. My branches reach up to touch the clouds and my roots go way down deep in the earth, drinking from the water under the ground.

Sometimes I am happy like the sunshine, and I make everyone smile. Sometimes I am sad and lonely like a gray cloudy day, and I just want to hide in a tree and cry. But when I cry my tears are like cool rain on a hot afternoon, and afterward I feel fresh and new. I know whenever I feel sad, scared, or angry, I can go to the earth and she will always be there for me. The rocks and creatures, the plants and flowers, the sun and the dark starry sky are all there for me. I breathe in the cool, fresh earth. I breathe out all my fears, my sadness, and my anger. I accept myself. I accept myself when I am happy and joyful, and I also accept myself when I have difficulties, when I am angry or sad. I smile to myself, and I see that I am a wonderful flower living on the earth. I am a part of the earth, and the earth is a part of me.

Invite the bell one time; children stand up.

THE STORY OF BUDDHA AND MARA

by Sister Jewel, European Institute of Applied Buddhism, Germany

The following story goes well with the song, "There's Ol' Buddha." It also works as an introduction to the Touching the Earth practice above. You can read this story aloud to the children.

TRACK 19

There's Ol'
Buddha

The Buddha was a person, just like you and me. Before he became enlightened, he was called Siddhartha Gautama and he lived in northern India and southern Nepal about 2,500 years ago. He had everything he could want: a beautiful palace, riches, the best foods, luxurious vacations, and plenty of power. But he wasn't happy. He knew something important was missing in his life. He still hadn't been able to tame his mind; he hadn't learned how to be peaceful, happy, and free. Anger, fear, and confusion kept him from being truly happy.

So he decided to become a monk and he went to live and practice in the forest. He had been practicing for six years when he finally felt he was near enlightenment. He had been feeling more and more peaceful, aware of his thoughts and feelings, and feeling much happier with his simple life. Now he was on the verge of completely breaking through his suffering to total liberation and happiness. That night, he sat down under the Bodhi tree and vowed not to get up until he was fully awakened.

But usually whenever we want to do something that is very important to us, we are met with challenges. Siddhartha sat in deep concentration under the Bodhi tree, and guess who came to disturb him? Mara. Mara is the opposite of the Buddha; Mara is the absence of enlightenment. If the Buddha is understanding, then Mara is misunderstanding, and if the Buddha is loving kindness, then Mara is hatred or anger. If we don't understand Mara, we can't understand the Buddha. Mara is inside of us, just like the Buddha is inside each of us.

Mara was determined to prevent Siddhartha from becoming enlightened. He sent his beautiful daughters to dance and the finest musicians to play for him. If you were Siddhartha sitting there as a young person, perhaps Mara would have sent an ice-cream truck passing by, or your favorite TV program, movie, or video game. Mara comes in many disguises, and when we really want to focus on something—like our homework, or building something—Mara may distract us and try to pull us away from what we really want. But do you know what Siddhartha did? He kept sitting peacefully, fully concentrated on his in-breath and out-breath.

Shall we sit beautifully like Siddhartha and breathe in and out quietly to help him resist Mara?

The Earth Goddess appears to support Siddhartha, sending Mara away.

And do you know what? The dancing daughters and musicians, the ice-cream truck, the TV program disappeared. That was Mara's first challenge: distraction and desire.

Well, you know Mara didn't give up easily. Next, he sent his army of soldiers on foot and on horseback, all armed with sharp spears, bows and arrows. They lined up in formation and all took aim at Siddhartha. Siddhartha remained solid and unafraid as arrows and spears whizzed through the air at lightning speed! Amazingly, as soon as they came near Siddhartha, they turned into flowers and fell at his feet.

Let's breathe in and out three times like Siddhartha to help him stay calm.

And guess what? With this, all the soldiers disappeared. Because when we are calm, peaceful, and clear minded, when we have love in our hearts, other people's unkindness doesn't have to hurt us. We don't have to let it wound us or make us angry and sad. If we know how to see that their arrows of cruelty, jealousy, and exclusion are really their misunderstanding and suffering, then we won't get hit by their arrows. Instead, they will turn into flowers that fall at our feet. That was Mara's second challenge: fear.

Mara wasn't finished with Siddhartha yet, because as you probably know, when we want to do something that is really important to us, the challenges we face can get very tough. This time Mara used his worst weapon yet: doubt. He himself came before Siddhartha, and with hands on his hips and head rolling, he shouted, "What makes you think you can be enlightened? Who do you think you are? You're just a nobody!"

This is a very unkind thing to do to someone—to make them doubt themselves. We should try our best to speak in a way that gives people self-confidence. Do you know what Siddhartha did when Mara questioned him like this? He wasn't shaken. He sat very still and put his hand down and touched the earth.

Let's all do that; sit with one hand in your lap and one hand reaching toward the earth. Let's breathe three times with Siddhartha, to help him get through this most difficult challenge.

Siddhartha calmly said, "I call on the Earth as my witness that I can become enlightened." And right away, the earth shook and the Earth Goddess sprang up from the ground in all her glory and splendor. She put her hand on Siddhartha's shoulder with all her support and love, and she looked at Mara firmly and said, "Don't doubt Siddhartha. He is going to be enlightened and help all beings find peace and freedom." And with that Mara vanished, totally defeated once and for all.

And sure enough, as the morning star appeared in the sky, Siddhartha attained enlightenment and understood that everyone has the nature of enlightenment but they don't know it. That means you and me. So this story reminds us that the Earth is always there for us, ready to support us and help us when we have difficulty.

Now we're going to practice Touching the Earth so that we can connect to the people and things that always love and support us. The Earth is so huge and powerful that we just have to lay our head down on her or reach down toward her, rest and relax completely, and we will feel her energy and strength come into us. Anytime you feel upset, lonely, scared, or confused, go to the Earth. Release your feelings onto the Earth and open yourself up to her support and healing energy.

WHAT AM I MADE OF?

MATERIALS: for each child, a roll of paper that is at least two feet wide and long enough to draw the child full-sized from head to toe; drawing or painting materials; old magazines; items from nature; glue (optional); and one pair of scissors (to be used by the adult)

This can be an interesting exercise to help the children reflect on interconnection and interbeing. You could have a discussion after the practice of Touching the Earth or Beginning Anew about all the things that make up who we are and what we need to survive. We can also ask the children about the different things they like [*foods, music, sports, the arts, friends, places*] and ask them to reflect on how these things also make up who we are.

Ask the children to get into pairs. Each pair rolls out one of the papers and one of the children lies down on it. Then you can cut the paper so it's just a bit longer than the length of the child. The other child takes a pencil or crayon and draws the outline of the child who is lying on the paper. Then the children switch places. After all the children have an outline of their body, ask them to draw inside the outline of their body some of the things that make up who they are: sun, water, soil, animals, plants, parents, food, books, games, etc. In addition to drawing, children can gather objects from nature, bring things from home, or cut pictures from magazines to glue onto their artwork.

An alternative art project is to have the children reflect on the time when they were in their mother's womb, connected to her through the umbilical cord. When they were born the cord was cut, but they are still connected to their mothers and fathers through a kind of invisible umbilical cord. And not only are they still deeply connected to their mothers and fathers, but they are also linked to the sun, the river, the trees, the animals, and the air. Without the trees we have no oxygen to breathe. Without the river we have no water to drink, so in truth an invisible umbilical cord links us to everything in the cosmos. Invite the children to draw, on 8½" x 11" (or A4) paper, pictures of themselves as a baby with many umbilical cords, connecting them to all the many things that sustain their life. For inspiration, read the story about being a tiny seed in a mother's womb at the beginning of this chapter.

7
understanding
and compassion

I vow to develop UNDERSTANDING *in order to live peacefully with*
people, animals, plants, and minerals.
I vow to develop my COMPASSION *in order to protect the lives of people,*
animals, plants, and minerals. —THE TWO PROMISES

THESE ARE THE TWO PROMISES, the mindfulness trainings or ethical guidelines
for children. In order to love, you need to understand, because love is made
of understanding. If you do not understand someone, you cannot love him.
Meditation is looking deeply to understand the needs and suffering of the other
person. When you feel that you are understood, you feel love penetrating you.
It's a wonderful feeling. All of us need understanding and love.

People like doing different things. Suppose that after school you and your
friend want to do something together. Your friend wants to play tennis; you
want to read. But because you want to make your friend happy, you put down
your book and go out to play tennis with him. You are practicing understanding when you do this. Through your understanding, you give your friend joy.
When you make him happy, you become happy, too. This is an example of
practicing understanding and loving.

Whenever you recite these two vows, ask yourself these questions: "Since
I have made these vows, have I tried to learn about them? Have I tried to

practice the vows?" I do not expect a yes or no answer to these questions. Even if you have tried to learn about the vows and have tried to practice them, this is not enough. The best way to respond to these questions is to open yourself and let the questions enter deeply into your whole being while you breathe in and out. Just open yourself to the questions and they will begin to work silently in you.

Understanding and love are the two most important teachings of the Buddha. If we do not make the effort to be open, to understand the suffering of other people, we will not be able to love them and to live in harmony with them. We should also try to understand and protect the lives of animals, plants, and minerals and live in harmony with them. If we cannot understand, we cannot love. The Buddha teaches us to look at living beings with the eyes of love and understanding. It is important that we learn how to practice this teaching.

Receiving the Two Promises

In our retreats, just before the adults receive the Five Mindfulness Trainings transmission, the children have the opportunity to receive the Two Promises in a formal ceremony. The children receive a Dharma name and a certificate to remind them of their promises.

Before the children receive the Two Promises, they are asked to write about their aspirations and why they want to receive them. Here are some responses:[*]

I want to take the Two Promises because it will make me more mindful, and the people around me will be happier. I also think they will help me be less nervous when I meet new people.
—Joanna S., Loving Home of the Heart, age 12

---

[*] From *I Have Arrived, I Am Home: Celebrating Twenty Years of Plum Village Life*, by Thich Nhat Hanh (Berkeley, CA: Parallax Press, 2003).

The Two Promises

I vow to develop UNDERSTANDING
in order to live peacefully

  with people, animals, plants and minerals.

I vow to develop COMPASSION

in order to protect the lives

  of people, animals, plants and minerals.

I hope the Two Promises will help me to understand my family's needs better. I also hope I can teach myself to feel compassion for other people and myself.
—Siena D., Healing Joy of the Heart, age 11

I would like to be more compassionate. I would like to understand myself and other people better.
—Djuna W., Radiant Smile of the Heart, age 10

Because they will help me be with people more easily, make my life happier.
—Nguyen An L., Peaceful Joy of the Heart, age 7

I want to have a memory of Thich Nhat Hanh because he is nice. He is fun with children, and I like singing and praying.
—Max M., Peaceful Strength of the Heart, age 7

I really want to understand and help other things. I want to be a veterinarian to help animals. I want to make sure that there are no more poachers in the world, plant a lot more trees and seeds, and help people that are suffering.
—Maeve K., Great Offering of the Heart, age 7

I want to receive the Two Promises because if I have understanding, then I can be respectful, nice, and helpful, and giving. If I have compassion, then I can love my relatives more, and I can also listen to people better.
—Ryah B., Generous Listening of the Heart, age 11

I want to receive the Two Promises because it will help me to understand my brother and sister when I water their seeds of anger and seeds of joy and compassion—to live peacefully with them.
—Hylan K., Skillful Gardener of the Heart, age 12

I would like to take the promises so I learn how to love others deeply.

—Mary Ann N., Precious Stream of the Heart, age 11

SHARING ABOUT THE TWO PROMISES

In every retreat, we share about how the Two Promises can help us in our lives. To explore what UNDERSTANDING means, we start by asking,

- *What does peace mean to you?*
- *How can we understand and live peacefully with other people?*
- *With animals?*
- *With plants and with the Earth?*

The children will begin to contemplate real situations that they have experienced or are experiencing. Sometimes a group of children might not be so talkative or responsive. In this case we can share examples from our own lives to illustrate the meaning of the qualities of understanding and compassion. It's good to have some stories ready to tell when teaching this practice. We can also share about caring for the environment and the Earth when we speak about caring for minerals. The children often have lots of ideas about how they can protect the environment.

We can continue to explore the meaning of COMPASSION:

- *Can anyone share what love means to you?*
- *What do we do to show that we love someone or something, like our moms and dads, cats or dogs, plants?*
- *How can we protect those we love, including animals, plants, and the Earth?*
- *And if we love our friends how can we show that? How do others show their understanding and compassion to us?*

As the group touches the beauty and importance of the qualities of compassion and understanding in daily life, you can introduce them to the Two

Promises. Share with them "The Two Promises" song. The song includes three breaths ("mmm . . . ahh . . ." three times) after each promise because we need that strength and mindfulness to keep our promise. The children love the hand movements that accompany the song. You can find them on the Planting Seeds website. You can then have them fill out the Two Promises Practice Sheet online to go even deeper and find their own concrete examples. They may like to make drawings that represent how they can express their understanding and compassion

in their daily lives. It is good to have a poster of the Two Promises on the wall of your room so everyone can remember them. Ask the children to decorate it. You can also play the song "I Love Nature" to reinforce their connection with nature.

The Mosquito Question

QUESTION: *Thay, mosquitoes keep biting me and I want them to stop it. Can I kill just a few every day?*

THAY: How many do you want to kill?

CHILD: *About one a day.*

THAY: Do you think that's enough?

CHILD: *Yeah.*

THAY: When I was a little boy I also had that question. Later on, I learned that a mosquito needs food in order to live. A mosquito is always trying to get some food. It is like us. When we are hungry we also look for something to eat, and that's very natural. I think there are ways in which we can protect ourselves from being bitten by mosquitoes. In Vietnam everyone has a mosquito net to sleep under at night. And if they don't use a mosquito net, they have to kill mosquitoes the whole night. Not only a few—because after you kill one, another will come. You could spend your entire night killing mosquitoes. So killing mosquitoes is not a solution. One way we can protect ourselves is by using a mosquito net. I think there are a few mosquito nets in Plum Village. You just ask and the brothers may let you borrow one, so you can spare the life of little mosquitoes.

Sometimes when I see a mosquito landing on me, I produce a kind of storm with my hand so the mosquito will fly away. I do it without any anger. I just prevent the mosquito from biting.

Stories about Connecting with Animals

Here are two true stories you could read to the children to stimulate discussion about the Two Promises and protecting animals.* Invite the children to tell their own animal stories.

A PARISIAN BODHISATTVA

Malakoff, a very large Newfoundland dog, was the watchdog for a Parisian jeweler. One of the jeweler's apprentices, a man named Jacques, hated Malakoff who, perhaps, sensed something about the man that he did not trust.

Jacques resolved to kill the dog.

With a few other cohorts, Jacques led the great dog to the River Seine, tied a stone around his neck, and threw him into the fast-moving water. Malakoff fought for his life, swimming and struggling for the shore. He swam so powerfully that even with the stone he managed to make it almost to the shore. Then Malakoff looked behind him and realized that his attacker, Jacques, had fallen into the water, too, and was drowning. The man gulped for air as he thrashed in the water but, not knowing how to swim, he panicked and started to go down.

Peaceful Kingdom: Random Acts of Kindness by Animals by Stephanie Laland (Newburyport, MA: Conari Press, 2008).

Seeing this, Malakoff turned and swam back toward Jacques. Despite the heavy weight around his neck, Malakoff swam, panting and straining, to where his would-be assassin struggled. In desperation, the man grabbed Malakoff's fur. By now too weak to pull the man to shore in the strong cross-currents, Malakoff struggled with all his might just to tread water with both the stone weight and the panicky man. The dog held Jacques afloat until others could rescue him.

Once man and dog were both safely on shore, the remorseful apprentice threw his arms about the great Newfoundland and wept as he begged the dog's forgiveness.

The story of the heroic dog spread throughout Paris. Malakoff became such a symbol of valor that when he died, nearly every apprentice in Paris followed his funeral procession.

GOOD SAMARITAN DOLPHINS

In June 1971, Yvonne Vladislavich was sailing on a yacht in the middle of the Indian Ocean when suddenly the craft exploded. She was thrown clear but the vessel sank and she was left completely stranded. Far from shipping lanes, there was no hope of rescue.

Terrified, she treaded water awaiting certain death. Then she saw three dolphins approach her. To her astonishment, one of them swam underneath her and buoyed her up with his own large body. Gratefully, she held onto the dolphin's sleek, smooth body. The other two dolphins swam in circles around her to protect her from sharks.

The dolphins carried and protected her through the warm waters for many hours until they arrived at a marker-buoy floating at sea. They left her on the buoy from which she was soon picked up by a passing ship.

It was calculated that from the position of the buoy and the position of her yacht when it exploded, that the dolphins had carried her and kept her alive through two hundred miles of dangerous seas.

THE TWO PROMISES PRACTICE SHEET

You can download the practice sheet from the Planting Seeds website or have children make their own with the following text:

THE FIRST PROMISE

I vow to develop **UNDERSTANDING** in order to live peacefully with:

write the name or draw a
picture of a person

write the name or draw a
picture of an animal

write the name or draw a
picture of a plant

write the name or draw a picture of
a mineral or a place that is
important to you—like your garden,
schoolyard, a park, or the beach

THE SECOND PROMISE

I vow to develop my **COMPASSION** in order to protect the lives of:

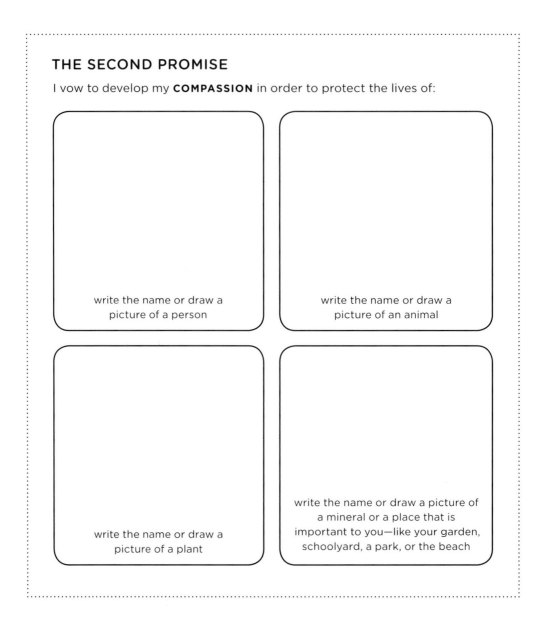

write the name or draw a
picture of a person

write the name or draw a
picture of an animal

write the name or draw a
picture of a plant

write the name or draw a picture of
a mineral or a place that is
important to you—like your garden,
schoolyard, a park, or the beach

Questions for reflection:

- *What were the acts of understanding or compassion in the two stories?*
- *How do you think the dolphins were able to be at the right place at the right time to come to the woman's rescue?*
- *Why do you think the animals in these stories wanted to help people they didn't know and even to help a person who was trying to harm them?*
- *Do you know any true stories of animals helping people or other animals?*
- *How can we protect the animals in our environment?*

Mindful Eating

EATING WITH COMPASSION

Eating and drinking can be very violent to us and to the world. If we don't know how to practice mindful eating, we can bring a lot of poisons and a lot of violence into our body and consciousness. Reading and watching television can also be very violent. This is why we have to learn to consume with mindfulness. Mindfulness can guide us and protect our body, our mind, and the collective body and consciousness of our family and all beings on the planet. In our family we may like to sit down together and discuss how to apply nonviolence in our daily life—in our eating, drinking, and entertaining.

Eating and drinking can be a deeply spiritual act. We can eat in such a way that we nurture our compassion and understanding, and only bring into our body what is nourishing and healing. We can eat in a way that helps the energy of compassion in us to arise and grow. This is a very deep practice. When we organize a session of tea meditation in Plum Village, or a lemonade meditation for the children, the act of drinking tea or lemonade in the spirit of brother-hood, sisterhood, joy, and harmony is deeply spiritual.

As we sit around the table, a young person can recite aloud the contem-plations before eating. The child can point to every dish on the table and tell

Food Contemplations

This food is the gift of the whole universe: the earth, the sky, the rain and the sun.

We thank the people who have made this food, especially the farmers, the people at the market and the cooks.

We only put on our plate as much food as we can eat.

We want to chew the food slowly so that we can enjoy it.

We want to eat in a way that nurtures our compassion, protects other species and the environment, and reverses global warming.

This food gives us energy to practice being more loving and understanding.

We eat this food in order to be healthy and happy, and to love each other as a family.

us about the origin of that food—whether growing that food has destroyed many living beings, whether the way of growing the food creates harmony and compassion.

We have to eat with discernment and with mindfulness in order to be able to see clearly and keep our compassion alive. I have learned during my life that someone who doesn't have compassion cannot be happy. Without the energy called compassion, we're cut off from the world. We're not in touch with other living beings. So we eat in such a way that compassion is possible. With our awareness of nature and living beings, we can learn to produce and eat food in such a way that life around us and within us is still possible. As we learn more about this every day, we can eat our breakfast in such a way that our compassion grows and our anger begins to diminish.

CONTEMPLATIONS AT MEALTIME

1   This food is the gift of the whole universe: The earth, the sky, the rain, and the sun.

2   We thank the people who have made this food, especially the farmers, the people at the market and the cooks.

3   We only put on our plate as much food as we can eat.

4   We want to chew the food slowly so that we can enjoy it.

5   We want to eat in a way that nurtures our compassion, protects other species and the environment, and reverses global warming.

6   This food gives us energy to practice being more loving and understanding.

7   We eat this food in order to be healthy and happy and to love each other as a family.

> TRACK 22
> ·····················
> Contemplations
> at Mealtime

In our retreats, the children enjoy reading this verse out loud for the whole community before we begin our meal. They also enjoy reading and practicing it before they eat their meals at home or school. You can listen to children reading these Contemplations at Mealtime on Track 22.

SNACK MEDITATION

MATERIALS: prepared snack, tray or bowl, napkins; cup of apple juice for each child; bell and inviter

It is important to serve healthy snacks, like fresh or dried fruit, nuts, pretzels, crackers, or cookies made from whole grains (without artificial ingredients or too much sugar). We can serve water or juice in reusable cups to avoid creating a lot of trash, and prepare basins of water beforehand so that each child can help wash their cup.

Place the snack and napkins on a tray or in bowls. After passing around the snack, you can pass the cups of juice one by one.

We have the chance now to practice snack meditation. As you pass the tray around, please hold the tray so you can serve the child next to you. The child you serve bows and takes a napkin and a snack, and then bows again and takes the tray to hold for the next child and so on.

Please really look each other in the eyes and appreciate each other's presence when serving each other. Please wait to begin eating and drinking until everyone has a snack. We will eat in silence in order to really taste and appreciate the food.

Ask a child to invite the bell once everyone is served.

Let's all begin together and enjoy eating and drinking our snacks in silence.

If you like, pass around the snack again for those who want seconds.

Let's look deeply together into the snacks. How does it feel to eat quietly?

[Weird; I like it; funny]

How is it different from eating with the TV or music on or while doing our homework?

[I enjoy the food more when I eat it this way]

Why did you enjoy the snack?

What part of the snack do you think took the longest amount of time to grow?

Which food traveled the farthest to reach us?

Did you taste the sun in our snack? What else did you taste?

[The rain, the truck driver, the worms that aerated the soil]

So all these are part of our snack and juice . . . and they become a part of us when we eat and drink them.

Let's look into our apple juice. How long does it take for an apple to grow?

[From spring to fall; a few months]

Well, technically it only takes several months for an apple to grow from a blossom to a fruit, but before that the tree has to have grown for several years. A tree cannot bear fruit in the first years. So you could say the apple is several years old, not just a few months.

And before the "mother tree" was there, it had to have come from the "grandmother tree," so it's possible to say the apple is the age of the grandmother tree, and on and on, back to the very first apple.

So actually the apple we are eating is thousands and thousands of years old! Looking at it that way makes it pretty special to eat a piece of apple! And after all those years, we eat it in just a few seconds!

Since the apple took so long to come to us, it's nice to take our time to enjoy it. We can learn to eat all of our food this way.

When we establish this way of eating as a kind of ritual and we repeat it regularly, the children get used to it and come to expect it. It is a calming time in the day, a time when we experience togetherness and concentration. When asked what they liked the most about the Children's Program, some children said the Snack Meditation!

TRACK 23
Many Hands

TRACK 24
Little Tomato

You can teach the children the song "Many Hands" to help them appreciate all the elements that go into our food. They may also enjoy listening to the song "Little Tomato."

Ninth Graders' Reflections on Orange Meditation*

YEON JU: "At first I wasn't exactly sure why we were to put so much thought into just an orange. Plainly, there were the orange pickers, the farmers, and the market owners selling the oranges. However, when reminded of Thay's poem that we read in class about how, in order for this paper to be made, rain had to fall for the tree to grow, I was then able to concentrate on the deep meaning of the activity, which was to get out of the trance of thinking that the orange is a simple matter and should have been in my hands without the effort and natural process of a thousand events. Before the orange pickers, or even the farmers who planted the orange tree, the Earth had to exist. It may sound like an exaggeration to think about prehistoric times just for an orange to have happened. But like all humans, the current existence of you and me took just as much time.

In conclusion, I learned that we shouldn't take things for granted, but actually think about how they came to be, and how much effort and time was put into just one simple thing. And I learned to be thankful, thoughtful, and simply more aware of my surroundings."

AKASH: "When we eat food at home, we don't think of what people went through just so we could enjoy our food. When we started eating the orange, I was actually thinking about what people did, and for the first time in my life, I

---

* Students from Meena Srinivasan's class at the American Embassy School in Delhi, India.

felt as though I was thanking people I didn't even know. This helped me realize how fortunate I am. It also made me think about how everything we eat and drink starts off as such a little thing and how we are dependent on other people in order to get our supply of food."

RAISIN MEDITATION

MATERIALS: a raisin, or bite-size piece of fruit, for each child

There are many kinds of meditation. Now we have the chance to practice raisin meditation.

Pass out the raisins. Children should take one and hold it without eating it.

Please hold the raisin. Smell it. Notice its color. Feel its texture. Close your eyes and breathe while I invite one sound of the bell.

Awaken, then invite the bell.

Keeping your eyes closed, and in silence, very slowly eat the raisin. Notice all the sensations: Notice how it tastes. Pause. *Notice where you taste it on your tongue.* Pause. *Notice how it feels between your teeth and going down your throat.* Pause. *Can you feel it in your stomach?*

After you see they have finished, invite another sound of the bell.

Please open your eyes. What did you notice? How does it feel to eat something slowly and with all your attention? How is it different from our usual way of eating? Now that we've eaten the raisin, what has become of it? Where has it gone?

What are all the things that make up a raisin? Record their responses on the board. Help them see the interbeing nature of the raisin—it is made of rain, the cloud, sunshine, the people who picked it. Then guide them to look into our own interbeing nature by asking, *And what about us; what makes up each of us?* Again, write their responses on the board.

[We are made up of our parents, the food we eat, the books we read, the air we breathe, the water we drink.]

Look for the many ways that we and the raisin are interconnected. Invite the children to write a poem about the raisin, using the words on the board.

I AM IN YOU AND YOU ARE IN ME (MAKING PEANUT BUTTER BALLS)

INGREDIENTS: peanut butter, dried oatmeal, honey, sunflower seeds. Any or all of these: cinnamon, raisins, dried cherries, pumpkin seeds, chocolate chips, coconut flakes, dried date pieces, chopped almonds. If children are allergic to peanuts, sunflower seed butter can be used instead.

KITCHENWARE: big bowl, cookie sheets or trays, napkin for each person, refrigerator (optional)

First we need to wash our hands. We have two short poems we can say when we wash our hands. Read the gatha while the children wash their hands.

Turning on the Water

Water flows from high in the mountains.
Water runs deep in the Earth.
Miraculously, water comes to us,
and sustains all life.

Washing your Hands

Water flows over these hands.
May I use them skillfully
to preserve our precious planet.

Prepare the peanut butter balls (or follow the directions below for making the oat-carrot-carob-raisin balls). Combine all ingredients. Add the dry oatmeal to thicken, the honey to make it thinner. Taste to see if they're delicious. Add more ingredients if you like.

When the dough is just right, pinch off a piece and roll it between your hands until it forms a ball about the size of a ping-pong ball. Wet your hands to keep the dough from sticking. The children might like to invent a gatha for doing this. Place each ball on a cookie sheet. When all of the dough has been formed into balls, put the cookie sheet in the refrigerator to chill until it is time to serve.

Alternate Recipe: Oat-Carrot-Carob-Raisin Balls

INGREDIENTS: 1 cup oats, 1 cup shredded carrots, ½ cup carob/cocoa powder, ½ cup raisins, apple juice, finely ground nuts of any kind (optional), coconut flakes

Peel and shred carrots beforehand. Stir all dry ingredients together, except coconut flakes. Pour in enough apple juice so the batter holds together and is thick and firm, but not too dry. Form into balls. Spread coconut flakes on a plate. Then roll some of the balls in the coconut flakes until completely covered. Serve some with and some without coconut flakes.

Can you see a cloud in our peanut butter balls? Can you see a big truck? Can you see a lot of different people in our peanut butter balls? If you look deeply, you can see all of these things—and everything else as well! Let me help you look. What is peanut butter made of?

[*Peanuts*]

Where do peanuts come from?

[*Plants*]

What do peanut plants need to grow?

[*Air, water, soil, light*]

Where does the peanut plant get the water it needs to grow?

[Rain]

Where does rain come from?

[Clouds]

Aha! So that means there are clouds in our peanut butter balls, right? We could not have peanut butter balls if we did not have clouds, could we? I said that I can also see a big truck in our peanut butter balls. Do you see it now, too? Can you explain how it got there? (Accept all responses that show interbeing, for example, "Trucks have to bring the nuts from the farm to the grocery store.")

What else do you see in our peanut butter balls? This should be a very lively discussion! There is, of course, nothing that is not in the peanut butter balls, so all answers are right answers! [*I see Brazil because the cocoa that our chocolate chips are made from comes from there. I see the sunshine because sunflowers need sun. I see the people who picked the peanuts.*] Continue the discussion until there are no more suggestions, or until someone realizes that everyone and everything is in everyone and everything, that the all is in the one.

Why is it important to know that everyone and everything is a part of everything else? Why do we need to be able to see the cloud and big truck and all people and all those other things, including ourselves, in our peanut butter balls and in each other?

[*So that we will remember to take care of all things. So we don't feel lonely. So we will love all people.*]

DRAWING INTERBEING

MATERIALS: paper, drawing supplies

Either individually or collectively, you can make a poster in which you draw or paint a cookie, apple, raisin, or some snack food that you eat together regularly, in the center of the sheet. Have the children draw around it all the things that make that food possible: the sun, rain, the earth, plants, farmers, animals, etc.

Post it in the room to help everyone remember the interbeing nature of the food we eat.

8

cooperative games and enjoying nature

IT'S POSSIBLE to teach children to be mindful at a very early age. We can focus their attention on something beautiful, refreshing, and healing. If we are truly mindful and concentrated on something, the child will follow and focus her attention on it also.

Children are capable of seeing the beauty of a flower, a drop of dew, or a rainbow. It's easier for children to be in the present moment than for adults. They don't think as much about the future or the past as we do, so we can easily draw their attention to something in the present moment. You may take the hand of your child in yours and draw the child's attention to your joined hands. Your hand may be much larger and his may be tiny. You and the child can just enjoy contemplating your two hands.

Organized Play and Games

Games and play are fundamental in any children's program. The emphasis in our practice centers is on what we are nourishing in the children with the games—joy, fun, togetherness, lightness, and sharing. We de-emphasize the importance of winning and losing, and intense competition. At the start of the game we gather the children and emphasize that the purpose of the game is to have fun, develop our skills, and enjoy being together.

When preparing for games, choose an activity that you enjoy and also one that corresponds to the children's energy level at that time. Be flexible and prepare three or four activities, even if you are only going to use one. Then you can choose the most appropriate one for that particular moment. Do not hesitate to adapt activities to suit your group. Give the children and their needs precedence in any activity. At times, deep listening and loving speech, kindness and care, may be more beneficial than a game. More games are on the Planting Seeds website.

Cooperative Games

NAME GAMES

MATERIALS: small ball or a ball of string

HOT POTATO: Go around the circle asking everyone to say their name. Then present a ball, saying it is a hot potato. The first time you play, say your name and throw the ball to someone else as quickly as possible. The person who catches it says his or her own name and passes it as quickly as possible. Once everyone has had a turn, you make the game more difficult by saying the name of the person you are throwing it to; the person who catches it and must quickly throw it to someone else and say their name. Make sure everyone gets a turn.

MEMORY GAME: Going around the circle, say your name and one thing you like that begins with the same letter as the first letter of your first name. (For example, "I'm Gustavo and I like grapes.")

Now try it as a memory game, with one person building on the previous person's sharing, repeating everyone's name and what they like. (For example,

"He is Gustavo and he likes grapes. She's Laura and she likes lemon pie. He is Chris and he likes chocolate.")

IMAGINARY BALL

The children stand in a circle. They have an imaginary ball, an energy ball that has the power to be anything they want it to be. The leader starts by holding the energy ball between her two hands and then transforming it, through motions and gestures, into whatever she likes (for example, playing an instrument, playing a sport, being an animal, doing her favorite activity). While acting this out, she is not allowed to speak. Then the leader brings the energy back into a ball between her hands and passes it to someone else in the circle who "catches" the imaginary ball and subsequently turns it into something they like. This person passes it to the following person, and the game continues until everyone has had a turn. This game is silent. We show through gestures, not words.

REFLECTION: *How did it feel to "catch" someone else's "ball" and shape it into your own activity?*

FAMILY PORTRAIT

This is a game that can help us get to know each other's families. Have all the children think of their happiest moment with their family and take a picture of this moment in their mind's eye. Then, taking turns, each child gets to create this photograph, using the other children. He selects a child to be his father, another to be his mother, others to be his siblings, and another to be himself in the photo. Each child takes a still position that enacts whatever activity that person was doing in that moment. Once the photo is complete, he can share with the group what his happiest moment was. Make sure everyone has a turn.

REFLECTION: *How was your experience of playing different family members? And how was it to experience your family portrayed by other children?*

MARBLE ROLL

MATERIALS: empty paper towel or toilet paper roll for each child, one marble for the group

The children stand in a line, close together. Each child holds an empty paper towel or toilet paper roll. The child at the head of the line puts the marble in her paper towel roll and tilts it slightly so that the marble rolls into the roll of the person next to her. The object is to try to move the marble from the first person in the line to the last person without dropping the marble. No catching with hands allowed! If someone drops the marble, she must start over again at the beginning of the line.

REFLECTION: *What worked to keep the marble rolling? What didn't?*

Engaging All the Senses

The following activities and the reflections help develop mindfulness and concentration.

WHO AM I?

Divide children into two or more groups of three to five children each. One group of children stands behind a curtain. One child from the group sticks out only her hands, or one finger, or one fist, or toes! Or she just says a word. Or she sings a line from a song, or she whistles a tune, or claps her hands. The children outside the curtain guess which child is "performing." The other children behind the curtain get a turn. Then the groups switch places.

REFLECTION: *How could you tell who was performing? What senses did you use to discover this? Can you recognize a friend by only hearing the sound of her voice? Can you recognize someone by only hearing the way he whistles or sings?*

WHO ARE YOU?

MATERIALS: 1 blindfold

One child is blindfolded. The others stand still somewhere nearby. The blindfolded child moves slowly around the room until he meets someone. He tries to recognize the person by feeling only with his hands.

REFLECTION: *What senses helped you understand who you were touching? How did it feel to do this exercise?*

HUMAN CAMERA

Have the children get into pairs: One child is the camera; the other is the photographer. The photographer walks behind her "camera," with hands on her camera's shoulders. She carefully guides her partner, who keeps his eyes closed. She will have the chance to make three photos. She can guide her camera to just the right spot, either lifting his head up or down, to get the right angle. When she's ready to take the picture, she gently squeezes her partner's shoulders. He can open his eyes momentarily, and his partner can "take the picture." Then he must close them again right away. After the third snapshot, have the partners switch.

REFLECTION: *What things did you take pictures of? What was it like to be the photographer and the camera? Which role did you like better? Why?*

CLOUD MEDITATION

Lie back on the earth and look at the clouds. Take your time. Use your imagination. Be inventive. Imagine characters, adventures.

REFLECTION: *What did you see? Did a story come to you? Did you feel like you were in a different world? How long did each cloud hold its shape? Relax and breathe deep down into your belly. Feel the earth supporting you, and think about how you are a part of the clouds, the earth, and everything around you.*

FIND YOUR STONE*

MATERIALS: stones of about the same size, one for each child (stones should be about the size of a child's palm)

The children close their eyes and are given a stone to feel for one minute. They keep their eyes closed while you take the stones back and put them in the center of the circle. The children must now find their stone with their eyes open. Variation: After the children have had one minute to feel their stones, take the stones back and have them keep their eyes closed. Begin passing the stones around the circle, while students feel all of them with their eyes closed until they receive their own stone.

REFLECTION: *How did you feel doing this activity? How did you find, or miss finding, your own stone? How did your hands feel?*

WHAT DID YOU SEE?

MATERIALS: tray, napkin or small towel, ten to fifteen small, easily-identifiable everyday objects

Collect things like scissors, scotch tape, a CD, a watch, a cup, a fork, a piece of fruit, a paperclip, a stapler, a ruler, a flower, or a teabag. Place them all on a tray and cover them with a napkin. When all the children are ready, remove the napkin for twenty to thirty seconds (depending on the number of items on the tray and the age of the children). Then cover the tray again and see how many items each child can remember. This can also be played in teams. Each team can write down the items they remember, trying to get as complete a list as possible.

REFLECTION: *What tools did you use to remember the items? What worked, what didn't?*

Everyone Wins!: Cooperative Games and Activities by Josette Luvmour (Gabriola Island, B.C., Canada: New Society Publishers, 2007).

WHAT DID YOU SMELL?

> MATERIALS: a small tray; five or six fragrant objects like cinnamon, a lemon, mint, and other strong smelling herbs and spices; a blindfold for each child

Blindfold the children and pass around one of the fragrant items. The children are only allowed to hold the tray; they can't pick up the item (unless it's a spice in a spice bottle). Ask the children to silently guess what they are smelling, but don't remove the blindfold. When the object has gone all the way around the circle, they can share their guesses. When all fragrant objects have been passed around the circle, remove the blindfolds.

REFLECTION: *What did you identify? What did it feel like to smell without being able to see?*

WHAT DID YOU TOUCH?

> MATERIALS: several objects with varying textures, such as a cotton ball, a pinecone, some sandpaper, a smooth stone; a blindfold for each child

Blindfold the children and pass around one of the objects, starting with something soft, like a cotton ball. Ask the children to guess what it is. Next, pass around something prickly, like a pinecone, then something rough, like sandpaper. Finally, pass something smooth, like carved wood or a stone. Ask the children to silently guess what it is, but don't remove the blindfolds. When the object has gone all the way around the circle, the children can share what they think it is. After all objects have been passed around the circle, take off the blindfolds and allow the children to see if their perceptions matched reality.

REFLECTION: *How did it feel? How did you make your guesses?*

WHAT DID YOU TASTE?

MATERIALS: small pieces of several different kinds of fruit

Prepare different kinds of fruit, with enough pieces of each for each child. Have them eat the fruit with their eyes blindfolded or closed. Once everyone has finished, ask them to guess what it is.

REFLECTION: *Were you surprised? How was it different from eating with your eyes open?*

WHAT DID YOU HEAR?

MATERIALS: a variety of objects that you can make interesting sounds with, like a bell and inviter, a whistle, a stone to drop into water, a chalkboard to scratch, two sheets of sandpaper to rub together, a hammer for hitting a nail; a blindfold for each child (optional)

Ask the children to close their eyes (or blindfold each child) and then make a sound with one of the objects. Ask the children to identify the source of the sound. After offering the sounds of several objects, make a sound yourself, such as clapping, clearing your throat, coughing, clicking with your tongue, or whistling. The children identify the sound, then imitate the sound themselves. A child can then choose to make a sound for the other children to identify.

REFLECTION: *Which sounds were easy for you to guess? Which were difficult?*

LOOK! LISTEN! SMELL! TOUCH! TASTE!

Have the children sit still for a few moments. Ask them to see how many things they can see, hear, touch, taste, or smell in one minute. After the minute is up, ask the children to share their experience. They can also write about it.

REFLECTION: *What things did you notice? Did you notice one sense being more dominant than the others?*

COUNT TO TEN

The children sit or stand in a circle. The group counts from one to ten. Anyone can say a number, but if two people say a number at the same time, everyone has to start again from the beginning. This can be difficult, but it is worth persisting. It builds concentration, togetherness and awareness of each other. It's also a good game for quieting and calming the group. It sometimes helps if the group stands in a tight circle, shoulder to shoulder, and if the children close their eyes.

REFLECTION: *What did you learn from this activity? What strategies helped us get up to ten?*

Connecting with Nature

The song "I Love Nature" is wonderful to include in all of these nature activities.

TRACK 21

I Love Nature

SCAVENGER HUNT

Individual children, groups of children, or families can do this activity. Give each person, group, or family a set of small cards with pairs of opposites written on them. For example, soft and hard; new and old; wild and tame; familiar and strange; dark and light; etc. Ask them to find things outdoors that correspond with each card. Everyone shares what they found for each category and why they chose it. Encourage everyone—parents and children—to share.

ASKING NATURE'S PERMISSION

During a walking meditation or a hike, invite children to find a place outside to which they are drawn.

Invite them to approach this place in silence and to ask for permission to sit and just be there. They listen for a few moments to see how nature responds. They may receive a "yes" or a "no." If the response is no, they can find another spot and ask again. You can explain that nature sometimes gives us a no because the area is not safe for us or something in that area needs protection. If they receive a yes, they spend a few minutes sitting quietly in the area they have chosen. Come back together and ask them to share their experience. What attracted them to that spot? How did they feel nature's response?

Some of the things that people have shared representing a yes answer for them are a soft breeze, the song of a bird, or a warm feeling in their chest. Some have shared that no answers were a sharp or sudden sound or an uncomfortable physical feeling, like getting stung by nettles or caught on thorns. There are no right or wrong experiences. The exercise is simply to build awareness of and to cultivate respect for nature. It helps us recognize that we are part of nature and not the masters of it.

SEEING NATURE'S BEAUTY IN US[*]

Take the children to a spot outside and ask them to look around and see what they find beautiful. Ask them to choose one thing in their environment—whether it's a tree, a pinecone, a mountain, a cloud, an animal, another person, or a breeze—that they appreciate.

Give them each a small piece of paper and a pen or pencil. Invite them to write down: "I love . . . [the part of nature they have chosen] because . . . ." Or " . . . [the part of nature they have chosen] is beautiful because . . . ." They can write one or two sentences, something very simple. (For example, "I love the cypress tree because it is strong, fragrant, proud, and at ease with itself.")

Once they have written their sentences, ask them to turn over their paper and write the exact same sentence, substituting themselves for the part of nature

---

★This and the previous activity are from Michael J. Cohen, *The Web of Life Imperative: Regenerative Ecopsychology Techniques that Help People Think in Balance with Natural Systems* (Bloomington, IN: Trafford Publishing, 2003).

that they chose. (So, "I love *myself* because I am strong, fragrant, proud, and at ease with myself.") Then they can reflect on how it feels to recognize in themselves the same qualities they appreciate in nature. This can become a good reflection on interbeing and our oneness with our environment.

NATURE ALTAR

Go for a walk and ask children to pick up one thing that they feel connected to or that represents beauty, solidity, or goodness for them. It can be a stone, a leaf, a pinecone, or a flower, anything from nature. When you come back to your room, invite the children to share why they picked up that thing and what it means to them. Then they can walk mindfully to the altar and put it there. It's good to share a little about the meaning or purpose of an altar and ask the children if they have an altar at home. Now whenever they come into the room, they can bow to the altar and feel inspired by their item on the altar.

FINDING MY SPECIAL TREE

Take a nature walk with the children, looking at all the trees in the area. Each child looks for a special tree. When the children find it, they introduce themselves to their tree and tell it some special qualities about themselves. After awhile they can tell the tree what special qualities they recognize in it. Later they can share the message with their friends. Encourage the children to take refuge in their tree whenever they need it and to visit it every day. It is a safe place where they can just be, relax, and come back to themselves.

DEAR TREE, WHAT IS YOUR NAME?

Listening and looking deeply, being with the tree, and seeing all its wonderful qualities, the child can then see if the tree will tell its name. Or the child can give the tree a name. Children can then introduce a friend to their tree. They can share all the good qualities of the tree and why they like it.

DEAR TREE, WHAT DID YOU SAY?

MATERIALS: paper and pencil for each child

Children each sit at the base of their special tree, listening to messages from their tree and from the stones, insects, moss, bark, and leaves in the environs. They write this message on a piece of paper, or draw the meaning of the message. Then the children run to deliver this message to a friend's tree.

TREE POSE

Practice tree pose as in yoga. Stand upright on one foot only, the other foot rests on the inside of the standing leg; hands can come together at the heart or, with good balance, above the head. Notice the difference when you root your foot into the ground (even if you only imagine it). Notice what happens when you fix your eyes on a single point in front of you and concentrate. Children who cannot stand can raise their arms, placing palms together above their heads, and visualize themselves as a tree. What happens when you focus on your breath or on your abdomen? When do you have the "best" balance? You can teach them the song "Standing Like a Tree."

TRACK 25

Standing Like
a Tree

NATURE WALK ACTIVITIES

A PICNIC WALK: Everyone carries a small part of the final picnic.

STORYTELLING WALK: Invite a guest storyteller to join and have the group stop regularly to hear a story told in sections. Or tell the whole story during one long stop. Or have the children tell stories about nature they've prepared at each stop.

COLLECTING WALKS: Walk and collect special things from nature for the nature altar, for a poster, or for making cards or painting stones.

BLINDFOLD WALK: One person leads the other, who has her eyes shut. Then switch who leads and who is being led. (Have the children pay attention to light and shadow, direction, up and downhill, etc.) The guide can also lead the blind partner to touch a natural object and explore it with eyes closed.

LISTENING: Stand still, shut your eyes, and open your ears. What do you hear? Later, reproduce the sounds heard—cars, cow, cock's crow, bees, birds, voices, wind.

WALK BAREFOOT: Walk barefoot and pay attention to the soles of your feet and their contact with the earth. This is a fun way to introduce walking meditation.

NATURE MANDALAS: Go for a walk and choose a place to sit down. Notice everything around you. After awhile, make a mandala using the natural objects around you: rocks, leaves, flowers, grass, and soil. When everyone has finished, take a Gallery Walk so children can visit each other's work of art. Or together make one big mandala and divide it into sections, one for each child to decorate with natural objects.

Saying Good-bye

WEB OF LIFE

MATERIALS: ball of yarn

Children sit in a circle. Holding the ball of yarn, share one important thing about your time together. Then throw the ball to someone else while you hold on to your bit of string. The person you've thrown it to then shares. At the end, when everyone is holding their part of the string, a group leader can say something like, *Even though we are all going back home, we remain connected just like this string connects us now. We bring our time together back to our homes and our schools and we take each other with us as well. Then, we each create our own web of practice back at home. So, from this larger web, many smaller webs grow out from each one of us.*

Here are some other sharing topics for the good-bye session: Something joyful I experienced was . . . I remember when . . . I am thankful for . . . .

It is wonderful to have the children also share what they liked and didn't like in the program to improve the activities in the future. You could also ask them what they will take with them when they go home, what practices or things that they've learned. You could end with a group hug and singing a song together.

9

growing our happiness, embracing our suffering

WE ARE COMMITTED to a certain idea of happiness. We think that if we cannot realize this or that, if we cannot change this or that, then happiness will never be possible. Because of our commitment to that particular idea of happiness, we are not at peace with ourselves. We are trying to do something, to realize something; but maybe happiness is already there. All the conditions for you to be happy are already there. You only need to recognize them. But how can you recognize them if you are not present and aware?

Maybe you have not realized that the sun in the sky is a condition for your happiness. Just take one second to look, and you see that all life on Earth is possible because of the sun. All our food comes from light, from the sun. And when you look at the sun like that, you see the sun as your father, your mother— nourishing you every day. The sun is always there for you. You might think to yourself, "Nobody takes care of me, nobody loves me, nobody pays attention to me," but the sun is nourishing you every second, every day. The earth, the trees, the water, the air, the baker, the farmer, the birds, the insects, they are all there for you.

Those of us who have practiced stopping and dwelling in the present moment are able to touch the many conditions of our happiness that are available in the here and now. We find out that we don't need more, because these conditions are more than enough for our happiness. Stopping is very important. As long as you continue to run, happiness is very difficult. Stopping allows your body and mind to rest. Stopping allows you to recognize the conditions for your happiness that are already there.

The practice of mindfulness helps us to be happy right in the here and the now. We don't have to wait ten years to be happy. The moment we breathe in mindfully, we feel calm, fresh, and solid right away. We don't have to wait. Mindfulness helps us to be happy right now, today.

Cultivating Happiness

GIVING OUR HAPPINESS A CHANCE TO GROW

> MATERIALS: for each child: 1 clear wide-mouth jar or clear plastic cup (or cut off the top 1/4 of a clear plastic water bottle), 1 paper towel, soil, 8 lima or pinto beans; one permanent marker for the class[*]

We're going to plant some bean seeds.

Note: Demonstrate and help the children as you give them the following directions:

Let's name your bean seeds. One set of beans will be your Happiness Beans; you will name your beans after the ways of being that make you truly happy. For example, does it make you happy when others smile at you? Does it make you happy when you smile at others? If so, you might like to name one of your beans "Smile!" Other names for your Happiness Beans might be Mindfulness, Generosity, Freedom, Safety, Love, Hope, or Sharing.

[*] You can draw the seeds if you can't do this exercise with real ones; each child will need a piece of paper and a pen. Have all the children draw a circle to represent their mind and draw seeds in the circle to represent their emotions. Then, they can name each seed. Adapt the exercise and discussion accordingly.

What makes you truly happy?

[*Playing with my dog, being with my friends, sharing, irises*]

Your other beans will be your Unhappiness Beans; you will name your beans after ways of being that don't make you happy. For example, does it make you un-happy when you or someone you know is angry? If anger makes you unhappy, you might like to name one of your beans, "Anger." Other names for the Unhappiness Beans might be Selfishness, Fear, Sadness, Impatience, Hurrying, and Jealousy.

What makes you unhappy?

[*Fights, War, Stealing, Not Sharing*]

Wrap the inside of your cup with a paper towel. Carefully put soil inside the cup, on the inside of the paper towel. Fill it about 3/4 full. Place four beans between the paper towel and the side of the cup. Make a lot of space between the beans. Like us, beans like freedom!

Note: We use clear cups and paper towels so that children can watch as the beans grow roots and stems.

With the permanent marker, write the names of your beans on your cup.

We all have the seeds of happiness and we all have the seeds of anger, selfish-ness, fear, impatience, hurrying, fighting, stealing, and jealousy (and lots of other unhappy seeds!) inside of us. We don't need to judge them or push them away, but simply recognize them, and be mindful of them.

When the causes and conditions are right, our "seeds" grow, too. Just as with our bean seeds, if we give the happy seeds in us soil, air, light, and water, they will grow. Of course, if we give the unhappy seeds in us the things they need, they will grow, too! Just as with our bean seeds, we are the ones who get to decide which seeds will grow and which will not grow inside us.

What does it mean to give the seeds inside us air?

[*Freedom, space, time*]

What does it mean to give the seeds inside us light?

[*To notice our seeds; to shine the light on them*]

What are some ways we can water (and not water) the seeds inside ourselves?

With some guidance, these are some ways our children thought of to water or not water the seeds of happiness and unhappiness in us:

PRACTICE: "One way to water the seed of smiling is to smile a lot."

AWARENESS: "I water the seed of generosity when I notice that I am being generous."

DON'T CONCENTRATE: "One way to not water the seed of anger is to notice it but not keep concentrating on it."

CHECK MY PERCEPTIONS: "I can ask, 'Am I sure?' when I start to get jealous of a friend. Am I sure that what my friend has is what I want?"

BE KIND: "One way to water the seed of love is to tell our friends that we love them."

SAY A GATHA: "One way to water the seed of appreciation is to say the Contemplations at Mealtime." (see page 143)

BREATHE IN AND OUT: "One way to not water the seed of fear is to pay attention to our breathing."

TRACK 26

Happiness Is
Here and Now

DON'T WATCH MEAN TV SHOWS OR VIDEOS OR LISTEN TO MEAN SONGS ON THE RADIO: "One way to not water the seed of meanness is to watch only shows that are friendly and kind."

UNDERSTAND: "When I start to get irritated at my family, I can try to understand why they did the thing that made me irritated."

TAKE THREE STEPS: "One way to not water the seed of sadness is to take these Three Steps: 1. Enjoy things that make me happy. 2. Notice when I am sad. 3. Later, when I am not sad anymore, think about what made me sad and try to understand it and change it."

Teach the children the song "Happiness Is Here and Now." Invite the children to take their seeds home to care for.

WHAT MAKES ME HAPPY[*]

MATERIALS: old magazines with pictures, scissors, glue, crayons, markers, colored chalk or paint, sheets of paper for each child

We can say that there are two kinds of happiness: eating-sweets happiness and peace-inside happpiness. One comes from treats, like a new toy or a piece of cake. The other kind of happiness comes from a mind full of peace, like when you feel completely loved by your adults.

The first kind of happiness isn't real because it doesn't last, and it can end up giving us all sorts of problems. The second kind of happiness is more genuine, wider, and deeper, like an ocean.

Make a collage of the different things that make you happy, for example, eating an ice-cream cone or hugging your family members. If you can't find a picture, draw one instead. Color in the background of the collage, too, with a happy pattern.

When you have finished, make two lists: short-term pleasure and long-term pleasure. In which list do each of your types of happiness belong? On a new sheet of paper, make a larger drawing of your favorite example of happiness.

TRACK 27

Great Big Smile

Teach the children the song "Great Big Smile."

[*] The next three practices are from the *Rigpe Yeshe Study Pack for Children and Teenagers,* by David Rycroft.

CONTENTMENT

MATERIALS: a piece of fruit, a small glass of water, paper, and a pencil for each child

What is contentment? Contentment is being satisfied and grateful for what we have. With contentment, we can take the time to enjoy simple things; we can enjoy drinking a glass of water as if it were the most delicious and expensive drink in the world!

Discontent, the opposite of contentment, is when you always want something more, like when your mom told you two stories instead of one, and then you asked for a third; or when you've been given a delicious piece of chocolate cake but you want even more.

Eat a piece of fruit slowly and carefully, noticing what the fruit looks like, what it feels like, and what it tastes like. Drink a glass of water in the same way. Write a description of your experience.

When you have finished with this writing, make up a poem. Include the word "contentment" and some of the words from the above description.

LASTING HAPPINESS AND ENLIGHTENMENT

MATERIALS: a sheet of paper for each child, pencils, pens, markers, crayons or paints, card stock paper for making badges (optional), scissors to cut out badges (optional)

We all have the chance—you, me, everyone, even the tiniest insect—to develop lasting happiness. We can all become Buddhas because we all have what is called Buddha nature, the seed of enlightenment, in the heart of who we are.

Draw some shapes and patterns that represent your Buddha nature, the best part of you that is clear, present, loving, and peaceful (though most of the time we

forget about it). You can make a small version of your design that you can turn into a badge to wear, reminding yourself that you have Buddha nature!

sharing. . . . .

GRATITUDE

by Eric Reed

I was on staff in the Children's Program during a summer retreat at Plum Village. One day, a little girl about seven years old asked to go to the meditation hall to meditate instead of having free time. I said that she could. A half hour later she returned, glowing in spirit. I asked her what she had done for so long, and she told me she sat and named everything that she was grateful for. I asked her if that took the whole time she was gone. She said yes and began to share with me all the things she was grateful for. I was amazed.

Embracing Suffering

In many discourses of the Buddha, it is said that the lotus can bloom only in the mud. Looking into the lotus flower, beautiful, exquisite, perfumed, you can see the mud. You cannot grow lotus on marble. You need the mud. Your compassion, your love, can be nourished by the negative elements within your consciousness. This is the Buddhist way of looking at things. If you have never been hungry, how can you experience the joy of having something to eat? If you have never suffered, you cannot recognize joy and happiness when it is there. Therefore, suffering plays a very important role in our happiness. Thanks to suffering, we can develop our understanding and our compassion. If you have never suffered, you are incapable of understanding human suffering, and you can't have compassion.

We shouldn't be too afraid of suffering, and we should know how to learn from it. Then we will know how to prevent suffering from overwhelming us, that's all. We need to know suffering in order for understanding and compassion to be possible. The Buddha said, "This is because that is." If there is no left, there cannot be right. If there is no mud, there can be no lotus.

Looking for a place where there is no suffering is naive. The Kingdom of God or the Pure Land of the Buddha is not a place where suffering does not exist; rather, it is a place where there is understanding and compassion. And if there is understanding and compassion, suffering *must* be there, otherwise what would you feel compassionate about?

If I have been able to cultivate freedom, understanding, and compassion, it is because I have suffered. If I had not suffered, I would not have the freedom, understanding, and compassion that I enjoy, and I would not be able to teach this to my disciples. So let us look deeply into the nature of suffering and not be afraid of it. It can teach us a lot and help us to cultivate our understanding and compassion. Let us try not to run away from suffering. All organic gardeners know that they need the compost in order to nourish the flowers and the vegetables. So if you have suffered, it means you have a basic condition for happiness.

It is possible to experience mental darkness and still be happy. This is also true of the body, because we can never have perfect physical and mental health. Even when there is sickness in our mind and in our body, it is possible to live happily with this sickness. When we throw a rock into the river, no matter how small the rock is, it will sink to the bottom. But if you have a boat, you can carry many pounds of

STUDENTS SHARE ABOUT HAPPINESS AND SIMPLE LIVING

"Happy living is not necessarily based on having luxury materials. With simple living, we can also enjoy life and relax."

"I can live with very few electrical appliances."

"The resources of the Earth are not inexhaustible; we need to protect the planet."

"We don't need to make our lives complicated; we can let ourselves have more quiet time to reflect, to think about our life."

"We can reduce using things which will pollute nature."

"Living simply, that is true happiness."

rocks without sinking. Your boat is the community of practice and it contains your own individual practice. If you practice well, your practice can embrace and carry the suffering.

I remember when I was a young Dharma teacher during the war with the French, I had a fever every day, but no medicine was available. And yet I never missed a class. I was teaching young monks and nuns. It was my deep desire to bring up a generation of young monks and nuns so that they could provide society with a new, more relevant kind of Buddhist practice that could better deal with the suffering in the country. It was a great pleasure for me to teach these young monks and nuns. Although I had a fever, I could still teach. My happiness was large enough to embrace my pain. So even when you suffer, if you have the joy of practice and are supported by a Sangha, it is possible to stay afloat both physically and mentally. You don't have to sink into the river.

Just allow the suffering to be in you. Don't try to remove it so quickly. You can just recognize it and allow it to be there while you develop a new kind of practice and happiness. And one day, when your practice and your happiness have become strong enough, you will restore the balance in you. In the beginning it may be a little bit difficult. But with the support of a loving Sangha, it will get easier. You can ask the Sangha to help you hold that suffering and darkness in you. And one day, you will see the balance restored. Both the positive and negative emotions are of an organic nature. This is why the development of one means the shrinking of the other side. Simply cultivating the positive, without trying to change the negative, creates a transformation.

sharing . . . .

SOLID AS A MOUNTAIN

by Terry Cortes-Vega, Master School, USA

Dharma Teacher Chan Huy sits before more than sixty adults and six children, ages two to fourteen, at our weekend retreat.

"Please come sit with me," Chan Huy says and motions to the children with a smile. They gather around him on the dais, wiggling and giggling.

"How are you today?" he asks.

"It snowed!" Julia Kate, who is six, informs him enthusiastically.

"Do you call that snow?" Chan Huy grins. "It was so little!"

"But it was snow!" she insists. "I made a snowball and threw it at Alex!"

"Well," Chan Huy smiles at the children, "do you have any questions for me today?"

"I do," Eliana, a seven-year-old, says softly.

"What is your question, Eliana?"

"I want to know," she hesitates, and then continues, "What do you do when people tease you about your culture?" Chan Huy looks at the child. There is a long moment of silence.

"I'm trying to think of the last time I was teased," he says, finally. The children sit quietly, looking into his eyes, patiently waiting for him to remember.

After a while Chan Huy says, "I don't remember the last time I was teased. How do the children tease you?" he asks Eliana. She pulls the skin of her Chinese American eyes back. "Like that," she whispers. The grown-ups in the audience feel our stomachs tighten.

"What do you do when the children tease you like that?" Chan Huy asks her.

"I try to ignore them," she says, "but it's not easy."

"Hmmm." Chan Huy pauses. Then he asks, "Now that you've been at our retreat, what do you think you might do when the children tease you about your culture?"

Eliana thinks for a moment. We grown-ups are thinking, too. What would I do to help this beautiful child? What would I tell her to do? The room is filled with the silence of hearts searching.

Then Eliana says softly, "I think I would sing 'Breathing In, Breathing Out.'" The grown-ups take a deep breath. Some of us blink back our tears.

> TRACK 6
>
> Breathing In,
> Breathing Out

"Would you like to sing it now?" Chan Huy asks gently. Eliana nods her head. He takes the lapel mike from his jacket and holds it to her lips. She begins to sing. The grown-ups sing quietly, under the child's voice, in accompaniment.

Be a Flower: Helping Kids Deal With Teasing and Bullying

CHILD'S QUESTION: *Dear Thay, what should we do when other children make fun of us?*

THAY: There are many ways to practice. If you are a good practitioner, then you can go back to your mindful breathing and you just smile to the person who is making fun of you. You don't get angry; you just look at him and smile. It shows him that you are not affected by his attempt to make you angry. Although you don't say anything, your message is very clear: I have peace in me; I am not going to get angry. This is also a teaching for him. You can do that only if you practice in advance. At home if someone does something irritating, you go back to your breath. "Breathing in, smiling. Breathing out, calming." You just look at him and say silently, "Why are you doing that?" You don't say it out loud. You just look and smile, and there is compassion in you. You see that the other person is not happy and that is why he tries to express his violence and irritation. You know that people who are happy don't make other people unhappy.

Every time you feel irritation, you don't say or do anything. Just go back to yourself and practice mindful breathing. "Breathing in, I feel calm. Breathing out, I am not going to get angry." Keep smiling like a flower and you will disarm everyone. They will learn from you. Be a flower.

When you provoke a flower, when you call a flower mean names, what will the flower do? The flower will continue to smile to you. Be a flower. When someone comes and tries to provoke you, just practice, "Breathing in, I am fresh as a flower. Breathing out, I am solid as a mountain." You have the flower and the mountain in yourself.

Of course we all get hurt when people say mean words to us. This is natural. Make good use of the flower and the mountain in you, and you will not be as affected by what other people say. If you begin to practice at your young age, you will become a great practitioner in the future and you will be able to help so many people, including your children and grandchildren.

Of course being peaceful doesn't mean that you shouldn't take care of yourself and defend yourself! You should. It is very important that if you are scared at school, or there is someone who is threatening you or touching you without your permission, that you do more than breathe quietly! You need to be safe and take care of yourself wherever you go. It is very important that you protect yourself, get yourself to a safe place, and immediately tell an adult what happened. Ask an adult you trust for help.

Peaceful Sleep

CHILD'S QUESTION: *I have two questions. What do I need to do if I have a nightmare and I am afraid to sleep again? And the second one is, sometimes I have problems falling asleep.*

THAY: I have a few suggestions, though my answer is not complete. When you wake up after a nightmare, don't go back to sleep right away. You may like to sit up and massage yourself. Or you may like to stand up and do mindful movements to help your blood circulate better before you go to sleep again. Or you can drink a glass of hot water.

Be careful when watching television. Many of the images on television can give us nightmares, so we need to select carefully the television programs that we watch. Also, we shouldn't listen to stories that can give us nightmares.

The third suggestion is learn to do deep relaxation before going to sleep. Lie down, follow your breath, practice breathing with the song "Breathing In, Breathing Out," and allow your body to relax. That is the practice of directing love to your body and your consciousness.

Another suggestion is that adults can organize their daily lives so that they can be more relaxed in their way of speaking and acting. If a child lives in a peaceful, loving atmosphere and is protected from the elements of violence and fear in television, books, stories, and conversations, the quality of his sleep will improve.

Embracing Our Emotions

RECOGNIZING FEELINGS AND EMOTIONS

A group leader can start these sentences and the children can take turns finishing them.

My happiest time today was . . . If I could get a letter from anyone, it would be from . . . I am happy when . . . I am sad when . . . I am grateful when . . . I am angry when . . . I am peaceful when . . . I am afraid when . . .

FEELINGS CARDS

MATERIALS: 8–15 index cards, colored pencils, crayons, markers or pens

Using the index cards, children draw a picture of an emotion on one side. Each child can choose an emotion to draw: happiness, sadness, surprise, curiosity, fear, hurt, calm, etc. (It may be good to bring a sheet with a list or illustrations of many emotions for them to choose from.) Collect the cards.

Each child takes a card and mimes the emotion for the group. The other children guess what emotion it is. Or, each child chooses one card and explains why she chose it. Maybe this is how she is feeling today. The group leader can also read out the cards one by one and ask the children to demonstrate together what each emotion looks like.

Taking Care of Our Hermitage

One morning, when I lived in a small hut in the French countryside, I decided to spend the whole day in the woods nearby, so I prepared a sandwich, a bottle of water, and a small blanket to use as a sitting cushion. Before I left, I opened all the windows and the door hoping that the sunshine would dry everything inside of the hut. I enjoyed the morning very much, but in the afternoon at about three o'clock it became very windy, and black clouds began to gather.

I knew I had to go back to the hermitage because the door and all the windows were open. When I arrived, my hut was in a very bad condition. The wind had blown the papers on my desk all over the floor. It was dark, cold, and uncomfortable, but I did not worry. I knew exactly what to do. First, I closed the windows and the door. Then to brighten up the hut, I lit the kerosene lamp, because there was no electricity. I built a fire in the hearth and collected all the papers that had been scattered around, putting them neatly back on my desk.

When I came back to the hearth, the fire was very beautiful. Now the hermitage was warm and pleasant, and I enjoyed sitting and breathing in front of the hearth. Outside the wind was still blowing and the trees were swaying back and forth in the wind, but in my hermitage I felt warm, cozy, comfortable, and happy.

There are days when you don't feel cozy within. You don't feel good. You feel like you are in the hut with the wind blowing in and scattering everything all over. You try to say something in order to make the situation better but it makes the situation worse. You think, "This is not my day."

It's like the time I came home to my hermitage during the storm; the practice is the same: you have to close the windows and the door. The windows are the eyes, the ears, and the mouth; close them all. When you feel miserable, you have to practice as I did with my hermitage. You have to close the windows of the eyes and the ears. Don't look or listen or do anything anymore. Then light a lamp, the lamp of awareness, the lamp of mindfulness. Breathe in. Breathe out. Mindfulness is a kind of lamp that you can light inside of you. And you might like to build a fire inside to get warm. Go back to yourself, and tidy up the hermitage inside you. Every one of us has a hermitage and wherever we go, we can bring our hermitage with us. When we feel miserable, we can practice like I did with my hermitage. Go back into the hermitage. Take care of it. Close the windows and the door. Light a fire and tidy up.

It is possible to restore peace and happiness with mindful breathing and mindful walking. When you succeed once, you have confidence, so the next time you fall into that kind of mind state, you know what to do to feel happier and more comfortable. Our body is our hermitage. Our mind is our hermitage. It would be a pity if we do not know how to make use of our hermitage for our protection, our healing, and our enjoyment.

Belly Breathing

When a feeling of sadness, despair, or anger arises, we should stop what we are doing in order to go home to ourselves and take care. We can sit or lie down and begin to practice mindful breathing. The daily practice of breathing can be very helpful. A strong emotion is like a storm, and when a storm is about to arrive, we should prepare so we can cope with it. We should not dwell on the level of our head and our thinking but bring all our attention down to the level of our abdomen. We may practice mindful breathing and become aware of the rise and fall of our abdomen. Breathing in, rising; breathing out, falling. Rising, falling. We stop all the thinking because thinking can make the emotion stronger.

We should be aware that an emotion is only an emotion; it arrives, stays for some time, and then passes, just like a storm. We should not die just because of one emotion. We should remind young people about this. We are much more than our emotions, and we can take care of them whether we are feeling anger or despair. We don't think anymore, we just focus 100 percent of our attention on the rise and fall of the abdomen and in that moment we are safe. Our emotion may last five or ten minutes but if we continue to breathe in and out, we will be safe, because mindfulness is protecting us. Mindfulness is the Buddha in us, helping us practice belly breathing.

We are like a tree during a storm. If you look at the top of a tree, you may have the impression that the tree can be blown away or that the branches can be broken anytime, but if you direct your attention to the trunk of the tree and become aware that the tree is deeply rooted in the soil, then you see the solidity of the tree. The mind is the top of the tree, so don't dwell there; bring your mind down to the trunk. The abdomen is the trunk, so stick to it, practice mindful, deep breathing, and after that the emotion will pass. When you have survived one emotion, you know that next time a strong emotion arises, you will survive again. But don't wait for the next strong emotion to practice. It is important that you practice deep, mindful breathing every day. After about twenty-one days, when a strong emotion arises, you will automatically remember to practice.

You may save the life of a young person by transmitting this practice to them. If teachers know how to handle their emotions, they will be able to help students in their class to do the same. Some students are so overwhelmed by painful emotions that they can't learn. Giving a session of deep relaxation in class, teaching belly breathing, and helping students learn to cope with emotions is essential. I hope that this practice can be shared widely in the education system.

BELLY BREATHING IN PAIRS

In your own words, share the teaching on taking care of our hermitage and belly breathing above. Then ask the children, *Have you experienced such storms in your lives when you have been overcome by a strong emotion? How did you handle it? Have you seen other people going through an emotional storm? How did they deal with it? Now we will learn a way to breathe through our very strong feelings so that we can calm them down.*

Have the children get into pairs. One child lies down, while the other sits nearby and gently rests her hand on the belly of her partner. Together they can identify the in-breath and out-breath, perhaps counting up to a certain number. Then the partners can switch places. When they are finished, ask, *How did it feel to breathe this way?*

Now invite the children to lie down on their own, with their hands on their belly so they can feel the rise and fall more distinctly. Or they can use a book, or something else with a similar weight, so that they can feel it as they breathe and also see it rise up and down. After a minute or so, they can sit up. Ask them, *Were you able to stay focused on your belly and your breathing? How was it different from doing it with a partner?*

If the children practice this kind of breathing regularly, it will be easier for them to remember to practice it during an emotional storm. To end the activity, teach the children the "Feelings Gatha" song.

TRACK 28

Feelings Gatha

sharing. . . . .

SPIRITUAL EDUCATION IN HONG KONG

by Father Kwan* and Christine Cheung, Hong Kong

Based on my observation for the past several years, many Catholic schools only provide religious knowledge to students, but they pay little attention to the spiritual dimension of both teachers and students. So in 2008, when I was asked to do research on spiritual education by the Centre for Catholic Studies, I thought, why not take this opportunity to nourish the teachers and students by introducing practices that can transform religious education?

I launched a project by first introducing three Catholic contemplative traditions (Franciscan, Benedictine, and Ignatian) and secondly by demonstrating the mindfulness teachings of Thich Nhat Hanh. About thirty teachers got to attend half-day, full-day, or overnight retreats, where they had the opportunity to rest, reflect, and be spiritually nourished. Teachers were inspired by the practices and then learned how to apply them in their schools.

Two years later, we see that the project has borne fruit. This school year (2009–2010) eight more schools—Protestant, Catholic, and non-religious—joined the project. More than forty new teachers are receiving training. The project keeps growing.

Christine Cheung, a teacher at one of the Catholic schools who has introduced this spiritual education program, wrote:

"We see that students can calm down and enjoy the quietness. All of us need moments of non-doing and emptiness. The young people spend most of their free time occupied by electronic gadgets

---

*Father Kwan is a Catholic priest from Hong Kong who, after practicing in Plum Village, went back to Hong Kong and began teaching mindfulness to his parish as well as bringing it into the schools.

that make their body and mind very tired. This program gives them a chance to rest and get in touch with their own heart.

"During the sessions, there is no teaching, no intellectual material. Students themselves are the teaching materials. We help students be aware of their breath, body, footsteps, speech, and emotions. Then we provide the space for them to feel what relaxation is, to be at ease and peaceful. Transformation comes from self-awareness. Lots of students said that after attending the program they learned that they need to: go to sleep early and wake up early; learn how to relax themselves; and learn how to minimize negative speech.

"During the first 'Relaxation and Reducing Pressure session,' 120 students, with the help of teachers, were able to find calm and to relax. They suggested the school organize these sessions more often. We can see their desire to live meaningfully from students' journal writing for the program."[*]

---

[*] Sharings from students participating in the Hong Kong Spiritual Education Program appear throughout this book.

10
a loving classroom: healing difficulties

ONE DAY THE BUDDHA went to the woods to do walking meditation, and on the way back he picked up some *simsapa* leaves. At the entrance of the wood he saw a group of monks. He smiled at them and held out the simsapa leaves. He asked, "Dear friends, which are more numerous, the simsapa leaves in the woods or the ones in my hand?" The monks said, "Dear teacher, the bunch of leaves in your hand, compared to the simsapa leaves in the woods, is very little." The Buddha said, "Dear friends, what I know is vast but what I choose to teach you is very limited. I don't teach you all the other things I know because I don't think they are useful for your transformation, your healing, and your happiness. I offer to you only the things that you really need."

In the same way, we should offer our children first what they truly need, and if there is extra time, then we can offer them other kinds of knowledge. I hope that leaders in the field of education, including the Department of Education, will consider this. They need to know that teachers feel they don't have enough time because of the heavy demands of the curriculum. When students suffer deeply due to violence, despair, anger, and the lack of love, it becomes difficult for them to learn. Educators have to address this fundamental issue.

We know that each one of us has deep needs. The deepest kind of need in everyone is the need to love and to be loved. There must be a way to touch these seeds of love in the students. To love is an art. If the educator knows how to love, she will be able to help her students learn how to love and how to receive love.

A second kind of deep need is the need to understand. If we have a lot of curiosity, then we will be eager to learn. If we can touch these seeds in our students, they will want to learn. We won't have to force them, and then teaching and studying will become a joy.

When I enter the classroom, I always feel a lot of joy. When I see the faces of my students I feel happy, and they also feel happy because we share the same kind of desire. We should make the object of our teaching and of our learning into something joyful that touches the love and curiosity in the student as well as the teacher.

This is possible not only for the students but also for us, because we teachers also have the need to love, to be loved, and to be understood. We need to be understood not only by our students, but by our board of directors, our colleagues, our employers, and the Department of Education. If we don't feel understood, we cannot be happy and do our job well. People in the field of education have to learn to listen to each other and to practice gentle loving speech in order to help others to understand, to see our difficulties and our suffering. A school system can operate as a Sangha, a Sangha of educators. We can come together, express our concerns and our insights, and help others be aware of our difficulties.

Many of us are talented enough to organize sessions of deep listening in the field of education. We can elect a few members of our community to voice our concerns. We must ask people who are responsible in the field of education, including legislators and government officers, to come and listen to us. This is the collective practice of the Fourth Mindfulness Training concerning deep listening and loving speech.[*] We can identify wise people in the country who know how to listen—scholars, journalists, authors, poets, or politicians—and invite

---

[*]One of the Five Mindfulness Trainings, ethical guidelines taught by the Buddha. To read them, see www.plantingseeds.org and for a detailed commentary, see *For a Future to Be Possible*, by Thich Nhat Hanh (Parallax Press, 1993, 2007).

them to practice sitting and listening to us. A few dozen of them can listen to us share our suffering as educators and express the suffering of our students. The whole session can be televised for the entire country to follow.

sharing . . . .

A TEACHER SHARES HER SUFFERING

From a session of Deep Listening at a Thich Nhat Hanh retreat

I live in Brooklyn, New York, and I teach a class of third and fourth graders. I worry so much for my students. They're anxious and they have so much on their minds. I don't see many outlets for their fear and anxiety.

Sometimes in the classroom if it's really crazy, I'll just stop everything and say, "We need to stop for a minute." I turn off the lights and ask, "What's going on? Why is the energy so high? Why is everybody so crazy?" Then the kids will say to me, "I didn't get much sleep last night." "It was very loud in my building." "I was waiting for my mom to come home from work. She didn't get home until midnight." "I missed breakfast." We'll talk about it, and that really does help, and then we can get back on track. I find that if I don't acknowledge the students' anxiety or just say, "I have to get through this math lesson," then the lesson is gone and so is my opportunity to reach out to the kids.

And I guess, dear parents, I would hope that you can spend more time with your kids. From my perspective as a teacher, I think the biggest thing that can be done to help students is to deeply listen to what's going on for your children. They're very worried about you, and they're worried about themselves. We need to parent them together; we need to give them the language to express what they're feeling. We need to give our kids that outlet, those ears, that mindful listening.

The Classroom as a Family

The practice of meditation can no longer be done alone. We have to practice as a Sangha, as a community. We have to practice the Five Mindfulness Trainings as a nation. In the classroom there should be time for the teacher to listen to the suffering and difficulties of the students. That will bring them relief and allow them to be able to learn and receive what we want to transmit. Students should also have the opportunity to learn about the suffering and difficulties of the teacher. Teachers can share their suffering and their deep aspirations. A teacher or a senior student can play the role of a coordinator in order for dialogue and sharing to be possible. In that way we transform the classroom into a kind of Sangha, a community, a family.

The teacher and students may organize sessions where they can play together, enjoy music, walk and breathe together, or eat together. In this way we become a family. We have the ability to organize things so that we can transform our classroom into a family where communication, mutual understanding, and relieving suffering become possible. This will facilitate teaching and learning, so that education becomes joyful. Even if we don't earn much money as a teacher, we can still have a lot of joy in our job of transmitting wisdom and love.

What needs to be done in order for the class to be a happy place for teachers and for students? This is a *koan*, a theme of our meditation—how to help the children feel happy when they think of the school and the class? How can teachers feel excited when they think of their class? Teachers can use their talent and imagination and combine them with the talent and imagination of the students to make the class into a wonderful place to be together. This is possible.

Loving Support Groups

If there is suffering in the classroom, teachers can help the children form loving support groups to help understand and transform that suffering. Students and teacher may like to select two, three, four or five children to form a group. The purpose of the loving support group is to begin practicing peace in the class in order to bring happiness to all the children and teachers. After the original group of kids has had some experience listening, other children can take turns joining the loving support group and learn the practice of deep listening. Much of the suffering that students experience comes from miscommunication. So often, children don't feel heard or understood. With the practice of deep listening and deep looking, the path out of suffering will reveal itself to us. The practice of deep listening and looking deeply into our suffering can bring about a happy and harmonious class.

In order to transform suffering in your classroom, your loving support group may propose to organize a session of deep, compassionate listening. "Dear Teacher, we want a session where we can tell you all our difficulties, all our suffering. Many of us suffer in our family and in our class, and we would like you to know about our suffering." This is a very legitimate kind of request, and by listening to your students you already begin to practice the teaching of the Buddha—looking deeply into the nature of your suffering. The school administration should allow us to organize such sessions in which teachers sit and listen deeply to the difficulties and suffering of their students.

In Plum Village one summer, there was a young girl of about seven or eight who cried and cried; she suffered so much. She said she didn't know why her teacher made her suffer so deeply every day, why her teacher picked only on her; she didn't know how to stop it. Going to school was very difficult, yet she had to go every day. When the whole Sangha listened to her, many of us, including the grown-ups, cried. Many had undergone the same kind of suffering.

If you have a loving support group in your class, a child like this can come to the group and share her suffering. "I suffer; please help." Then the group will sit down and say, "We are ready to listen to you. Tell us of your suffering." Everyone listens to her story.

The loving support group can find ways to help her to suffer less. They may choose one or two children to tell the teacher of her suffering. "Dear teacher, I do not know why that child cries every day, but she says she suffers because of you. She really suffers, she doesn't want to blame you; she just wants to stop suffering. Please tell us what we can do in order to help her not suffer anymore." When the group comes and talks to a teacher like that and asks for help, I think the teacher will try to do something in order to change the situation.

Of course if the child is strong enough, he can say directly to the teacher, "Teacher, I do not know why you pick on me every day and you make me suffer. I do not know what I have done. Please tell me what is irritating in me and I will do my best to change." She can use that kind of loving language. But if the child doesn't have enough confidence, then the child can ask the loving support group to bring up the matter. This is a very peaceful way of settling things.

The teachers should also be able to tell the kids that they too suffer in their family and that it can be overwhelming if they also have to suffer in their class. If there is a loving support group in the class, the children can encourage their teacher to speak out and tell of her suffering. After the kids have understood the suffering of their teacher, they will be much kinder, they will know how to support her and collaborate with her. Without good communication between teachers and students, happiness will not be possible. The teachers will not have the inspiration to teach, and the students will not have the inspiration to learn.

CONFLICT ROLE PLAY

Have a child tell a story about a time she got into a conflict. If appropriate, ask the children to act out how the incident actually happened. Then brainstorm together to find ways it could have been handled more mindfully and peacefully.

Remind the children about coming back to their breathing and being aware of their emotions. Encourage them to leave a situation of conflict, immediately if possible, before they explode or whenever they feel they are in danger. When they are calm enough to speak about their difficulty with the other person, teach them to use clear "I" statements, and to take responsibility for their own feelings. To avoid using language that blames or judges the other, encourage them to describe specific actions or words that have upset them.* For example, I feel hurt and angry when you say you will share the toy/book/snack with me and then you don't. (Rather than: You are a liar and never do what you promise to do!)

Then have the children act out the conflict a second time using the tools you've brainstormed. If you come up with several good vignettes, you could string them together for a performance.

Role playing can also be helpful for parents and children, or teachers and students, to do together. Act out a difficult situation (like getting the child up in the morning for school, or getting the attention of students who continue talking) and then reenact it differently in a way that meets the needs of both parent and child or teacher and student. Sometimes it helps to have other people act out your difficulty.

DEEP LISTENING IN PAIRS**

It is very important to be able to listen, both to ourselves and to others. It is only when we can really listen to ourselves that we will be able to listen to others. What does it mean to listen to ourselves?

[Listening to our bodies and going to bed when we are tired, not pushing ourselves too hard, respecting our limits, etc.]

To listen deeply to another person is a real gift that can be deeply healing. Can you recall times when someone really listened to you? What did it feel like to be listened to this way? How could you tell the other person was really listening to you? How did that person show their openness and receptivity?

You could write on the board the qualities the children name that define deep listening. If they don't mention it, bring up the importance of not interrupting the other, of listening from the heart, without judgment or comparison,

---

*For more detail see books on Nonviolent Communication with children by Marshall Rosenberg.

** This is a good exercise for teenagers; it could be modified for children under twelve.

and of quieting the inner chatter and commentary about what the other person is saying, so that we become a clear mirror for them, reflecting back what we are hearing. Remind them that in deep listening, we listen with the sole purpose of helping the other person feel heard and accepted.

To help the children practice deep listening, have them get into pairs. Decide who will speak first. You could write three topics on the board, and they can choose one to speak about. For example, they could speak about a recent difficulty, something they are looking forward to, or how they are feeling right now. Instruct them: *Now we will speak from our heart, as much as possible without censoring ourselves. Just share whatever comes to mind about the topic. You will have two or three minutes each. While the first person shares, the other simply listens from the heart, putting aside any thoughts or commentaries, just being totally present for the other. Invite the bell to begin and end. Now switch.*

After both partners have shared, invite the children to come back to the group and share their experiences of both listening and sharing. *Was it difficult or easy? Did you feel really listened to? If so, how did this feel in your body or mind?*

Healing the Classroom Environment

We may need to conduct listening sessions on a wider scale, not just within our own class. The teachers listen to their students, and if one session is not enough, we organize a second or third session in order to hear everything the children want to tell us. Teachers can invite other teachers to join in and practice the art of listening deeply to the students. We can also invite the principal of the school to listen to the children with us.

The children have to prepare carefully in order to express themselves clearly. They should feel safe enough to tell all of their suffering—the suffering they undergo in their family and the suffering they undergo in school. If children feel that they have too much homework, they should tell the teachers and others who are listening. The focus of education should not be to sacrifice the present to achieve things in the future, but to be able to enjoy the present moment right now. If the present is misery, the future cannot bring happiness. The duty of teachers is to understand the difficulties, the suffering, and the aspirations of their students. Teachers may need many sessions in order to understand their students, and the school administration should allow them this time. This is truly teaching ethics.

The children should also express their intention and their desire to listen to their teachers because the teachers have suffering also, in their family and in the class. Some teachers cry because of the cruelty of the students. Some children have a lot of violence in them, and they entertain themselves by making other kids suffer. Sometimes they do the same thing to their teacher. They see the weakness of their teacher and they take delight in making the teacher suffer. That is why many sessions of deep listening should be organized to listen to the suffering of both the students and the teachers.

sharing. . . . .

CREATING SAFETY AND BELONGING IN THE CLASSROOM

by Bonnie Sparling and Uri Wurtzel, the Paideia School, USA

In our class of seventh and eighth graders, we spend three to four hours each day with the same thirty students. Our guiding philosophy is that any curriculum should begin with the children themselves, and then circle through issues and topics that bring them greater insight into themselves. Whatever the subject matter—literature, social studies, ethics, or writing—we want it to matter to *them*.

Students find meaning as they lead the discussions and ask each other both critical and personal questions. They openly address the issue of popularity, specifically looking at who has the kind of power that can make others afraid of them, and they also discuss ethical ways to respond.

Family, social life, and identity are central concerns for adolescents, so the students make these topics a central part of their curriculum. Over the years, they have developed a writing program and a court system that help them clarify many aspects of their lives and achieve the kind of conflict resolution that helps them become happier.

The writing program focuses on the crucial personal stories of the individual students, and it demands emotional honesty and a willingness to grow. They write stories about their lives that show each other who they are. Because suffering and conflict are often the seeds of growth that lead to awareness, they organize conference times with teachers or trusted peers to openly face their emotions. Their defensive masks begin to drop, anger reveals the hurt, and hurt transforms into love. These conferences help students gain perspective and insight on what previously might have been buried by the cluster of these emotions.

Upon completion, stories are read aloud in class with great celebration. The students then discuss the story and how particular moments resonate with their own lives. This process builds community, trust, and awareness of the fullness of the human journey.

In order for students to feel safe enough with their peers to open up so fully, they need to build trust. To this end, they have developed a constitution and court system that allows them to hold each other accountable for infractions of that trust. They support each other to understand the motives behind those actions, then work together to find resolutions. The court system acts as a powerful instrument for safety and fairness, and as a great leveler of status and popularity—the currency of social power and source of tremendous anxiety in junior high.

Not acting out in class, not saying something hurtful about someone, and not breaking the code of confidentiality are just three of the twenty laws the students have created and take very seriously. They work hard to uphold the system, to protect one another from any action that could discourage classmates from feeling safe, from taking risks in class, and from sharing their personal struggles with one another. When someone is accused of an offense, they can plead either innocent or guilty. Then the plaintiff and defendant speak in the student-run court, where the whole class listens both to their accounts of the situation and asks questions to help clarify motives and deeper roots of the conflict. Usually, the truth of a conflict is more nuanced and complex than it appears at first. Perhaps a girl's cutting remark in algebra class stems from her own self-consciousness about being a poor math student, or a boy's snubbing of a bookish classmate comes from his own experience of exclusion in early elementary school.

As the members of the class experience the safety, trust, and opportunity that this system creates, they no longer view the system as punitive and externally imposed, but as a tool to maintain openness, comfort, and closeness. It is wonderful to watch the sense of community, the freedom to be authentic, the chance to enjoy one another, and the power of empathy that the students gain over time.

Adolescence is synonymous with turbulence for most students, but because our students create the curriculum themselves, many of the problems associated with this age are resolved. This stands as a testament to what they really want: to develop honesty, accountability, conflict resolution, sharing and belonging, a sharp and curious mind, and a rigorous but natural work ethic.

When our students take the next scholastic leap to high school, we're proud and happy for them. They carry a more solid sense of self, a fuller capacity for love and strength, comfort with vulnerability, and deeper, more mindful connections with their fellow students.

sharing. . . . .

LOVING KINDNESS IN THE CLASSROOM

by Susanna Barkataki, Sequoyah School, USA

This is the way I begin each day teaching fifth and sixth grade. I tap into my breath, and then I envision myself, roots planted solidly and calmly down into the ground, head up in the infinite blue sky, tapping into the loving energy in the universe. I feel tranquility, freedom, gratitude, and happiness; then I channel this energy toward my students. I look at the children, say their names in my mind, and send words of loving kindness to them. I use traditional loving kindness phrases I have learned, sometimes modifying them for the situation. "May Miro be happy. May he be well. May he have confidence. May he enjoy the basketball game this afternoon." I turn my attention to each child one by one. "May Latika be happy. May she be free of her suffering. May she find peace."

When I am doing this in class with the students there in front of me, I smile a gentle smile at each of them in turn. They often seem to feel this energy and smile back at me, though I say the words silently in my mind. At home, I often can't help grinning with joy as I recall each child's face. I look forward to starting my workday with them. Sometimes, if I am feeling stressed or sad, it is harder to do this practice for others. I then turn my loving energy toward myself first. If I cannot muster enough joy to get further than that for a day or two, I know it is fine to take a break and care for myself.

This practice of sending loving energy to my students helps me to remember the heart of my role as a teacher and to bring more compassion and care into my day. Students can also offer loving kindness. I have watched students become bright and strong as they share their loving spirit. All of us can bring this love and joy into our own hearts, share it with others, and be open to receiving it.

sharing. . . . .

EMBRACING CHALLENGING STUDENTS

by Angela Bergmann, Germany

There are challenging students in every class, and you will always have to find your own way of working with them. I have found two ways that work for me:

First, I try to find one thing about that student that I like: something he does well or something we have in common, anything to be able to connect with the child. I find if I am able to do this, then I can build a relationship. I try to incorporate that point of connection into how I teach. For example, I had one student who shares my taste in music, so I encouraged him to bring some music (something I am allowed to play at school) to help us enjoy our sports lesson.

Second, I find someone on staff who really likes this student, and I discuss the student with this person in order to see his more positive qualities. If this person is willing, I invite her into the class to work with this student. This may change how the student feels about being in the class. Students can tell when I'm having a hard time with them, and this creates stress and tension in both of us. Having someone who likes this student come into class, and participate with both of us, gives us a new way of working together.

sharing. . . . .

WHEN THINGS GET DIFFICULT

by Tineke Spruytenburg, the Netherlands

Anyone who works with children remembers some who weren't easy to be with. Here are some ideas that may be of help:

Remain compassionate: Difficult children do not exist. There are only children in difficult situations. Their personal history or current situation may make them stressed and anxious, which makes it hard for them to listen and participate.

Create inclusiveness: Often just inviting the child to be near you while you put your hand on his shoulder or back is enough to create an atmosphere of safety; your mindful breathing and words support the child. Children who suffer often have a desire to belong somewhere. Give these children a special task—such as inviting the bell—to make the child feel appreciated, useful, and accepted.

Use do-language: Very often we ask children *not* to do things and in many cases they do not respond. This may be because it is not clear what you want them *to* do. So, instead of asking them not to climb a wall, you can ask them to keep standing on the ground. It takes some practice to use this kind of language, but the results are worth it.

Give corrections in private, praise in public: When correcting a child, try to be neutral and give the child space to explain what has happened. Often, children are capable of correcting themselves on their own. Water the wholesome seeds in the child by praising the child for taking responsibility for his behavior and help—if necessary—to find ways to make up with the people he may have hurt.

With a group of children who show disruptive behavior, acknowledge their discomfort and invite them to help improve the situation: You could ask them to think of other activities they would enjoy.

I remember a group of girls in the Children's Program in Plum Village some years ago. From the first day on, they all sat together in a corner of the children's room, talking to each other, using materials without asking, playing with each other's hair, etc. They didn't respond to questions, didn't participate in singing or sharing, and seemed completely uninterested in the program. The staff didn't know how to motivate these girls, and the girls probably felt our discomfort. After two days, a monastic sister who was helping in the program went to the children's room during the afternoon rest, knowing that the girls would be there drawing and chatting together. The sister shared her feelings and invited the girls to express their feelings about the program, while sitting together on the cushions making jewelry. This spontaneous group activity helped the girls integrate into the rest of the activities and turned out to be the beginning of what became a beautiful performance offered by all the children—including the girls—for the Full Moon Festival.

11

everything is connected, everything continues

WHEN YOU LOOK at the sheet of paper you are reading from, you may think that it did not exist before it was made at the paper mill. But the sheet of paper has been there for a long time in various forms. There is a cloud floating in this sheet of paper. If there were no cloud, there could be no rain, and no tree could grow to give us the piece of paper. If you remove the cloud from the paper, the paper will collapse. Looking deeply into the sheet of paper, and touching it deeply, you can also touch the cloud.

Has this paper existed before it was born? Has it come from nothing? No, something never comes from nothing. The sheet of paper "inter-is" with the sunshine, the rain, the earth, the paper factory, the workers in the factory, the food that the workers eat every day. The nature of the paper is interbeing. If you touch the paper, you touch everything in the cosmos. Before its birth in the factory, the paper was the sunshine, the tree. The so-called birthday of the sheet of paper is only a "continuation day." We should not be fooled by appearance. We know that the sheet of paper has never been born, really. It was there before, because the sheet of paper has not come from nothing. How can you suddenly become something from nothing? How can you suddenly become someone from no one? It's impossible.

You may also think that when you were born, you suddenly became something and that before birth you were nothing; that from being no one, you suddenly became someone. But actually, the moment of your birth in the hospital or at home was just a moment of continuation, because you had already existed in your mother for nine months. That means your birth date on your birth certificate is not correct; you have to push it back nine months earlier.

Perhaps now you believe that the moment of your conception is the moment when you began to exist. But if we continue to look deeply, we see that half of you was in your father, and the other half was in your mother. That is why even the moment of conception is a moment of continuation. Practicing meditation is to look deeply into ourselves to see our true nature, the nature of no birth and no death.

Imagine the ocean with its multitude of waves. The waves are all different; some are big, some are small, some are more beautiful than others. You can describe waves in many ways, but when you touch a wave, you are always touching something else: water.

Visualize yourself as a wave on the surface of the ocean. Watch as you are being created: you rise to the surface, you stay a little while, and then you return to the ocean. You know that at some point you are going to end. But if you know how to touch the ground of your being—the water—all your fears will vanish. You will see that as a wave, you share the life of the water with every other wave. This is the nature of our interbeing. When we live only the life of a wave and are not able to live the life of water, we suffer quite a lot. The reality is that every moment is a moment of continuation. You continue life in new forms, that's all.

When a cloud is about to become rain, it's not scared, because although it knows that to be a cloud floating in the sky is wonderful, to be the rain falling down on the fields and oceans is also wonderful. That is why the moment a cloud becomes rain is not a moment of death, but a moment of continuation.

There are people who think that they can reduce things into nothingness. They think they can eliminate people like John F. Kennedy, Martin Luther King, Jr., or Mahatma Gandhi, with the hope that they will disappear forever.

But the fact is that when you kill someone, that person may become stronger than before.

Even this sheet of paper cannot be reduced to nothing. You have seen what happens when you put a match to a piece of paper. It doesn't become nothing; it continues on as heat, ashes, and smoke. Part of the sheet of paper has become smoke and it has joined a cloud. We may see it again tomorrow in the form of a raindrop. That's the true nature of the sheet of paper. It is very hard for us to catch the coming and the going of a sheet of paper. We recognize that part of the paper is still there, somewhere in the sky in the form of a little cloud. So we can say, "So long, see you again tomorrow."

Age and Death

CHILD'S QUESTION: *How old are you?*

THAY: Well, how old are you first?

CHILD: *I am six, almost seven.*

THAY: Listen, I am going to give you a good answer. I am the continuation of the Buddha, so I am 2,600 years old.

CHILD: *Oh!*

THAY: I am also the continuation of my father, so I am 110 years young. I know that you are my continuation and I feel that I am in you, so at the same time I am six years old also. That is true, because I have been reborn in that child. He will carry me into the future. So I am quite young. I am six years old. If you look around, you see me a little bit everywhere. I have different ages. Okay?

Transcending Death

CHILD'S QUESTION: *Why do we have to die one day?*

THAY: Imagine there is only birth, there is no death. One day there will be hardly any place to stand on Earth. To die means to leave a place for our children. And who are our children? Our children are ourselves. Our children are our new manifestation. The son is the continuation of the father. The father, looking at the son, has the feeling that he will not die because his son is there to continue him. Looking like that you see that you are not dying, you are continuing in your son. And your son is not dying because he is continued in his grandson and so on. Buddhist meditation helps us to look deeply to see that there is no real dying, only continuation in different forms.

Look at the cloud in the sky. The cloud may be afraid of dying, but there is a time when the cloud has to be transformed into the rain. But that is not really dying. That is changing form. The cloud changes into the rain and the cloud continues in the rain. If you look deeply into the rain you can see the cloud. There is no real dying. You continue to exist in many other forms. The cloud can continue in the form of snow, in the form of rain, in the form of the river, or in the form of ice. One day the cloud can become ice cream. If the cloud does not transform how can we have ice cream to eat?

I am not afraid of dying because I see myself in my disciples, in you. You have come to learn with me and there is a lot of me within you. I am giving myself to you. If you have received some understanding, some compassion, and some awakening from me then I am continued in you. Later on, if someone wants to look for me, they just come to you and they see me. I am not only here [pointing to himself], I am also here [pointing to the children.] This is what I like best about Buddhist meditation. Buddhist meditation can help us to transcend death.

You know that death is very important for birth, for our continuation. In our body there are many cells that die every minute in order to leave space for new cells to be born. Birth and death take place in every minute in our body. If there is no death, it is impossible for us to continue in our body. That is why birth and death are linked to each other. Birth gives rise to death and death gives rise to birth. If we cry every time one of our cells dies, we will not have enough tears left. If every time one of our cells dies we organize a funeral, then we will spend all our days organizing funerals. That is why we have to see that birth and death take place at every moment in us. That is why the role of death is very important. That is the first answer. But the second answer is better. Looking deeply, you don't see birth and death: you see that there is a continuation. If you study more deeply, you will see more deeply.

No After, No Before

CHILD'S QUESTION: *What came first, the chicken or the egg?*

THAY: Did the chicken come first or the egg come first? This is a very interesting question. But because you are a student of meditation, you have to be careful not to answer it too quickly. You see, you have to look very deeply in order to see the answer. At certain times of year when you look at the lemon tree, you only see the branches and the leaves; you do not see any flowers or any lemons at all. But that is when you do not practice meditation. If you look deeply, if you are a good meditator, when you look at the lemon tree—even if the lemon blossoms and the lemons are not there—you can already see the blossoms and the lemons. They have not manifested yet because they need a few more conditions, like time, like rain, like the heat. So you cannot say that the lemons are not there. The lemons are there but hidden. The lemon tree and the branches, the leaves, the blossoms, and the lemons—they are all there together at the same time. You cannot say which is there first. The time of manifestation is different but they are always there, you see?

When you look into this flower, you see only a flower. But the garbage is already there. Garbage and flowers always go together. If you leave a flower without any water, in a few days the flower will become a piece of garbage. If you're a good meditator, you can see the garbage right now in the flower. It's not true to say the garbage is not yet there. It is inside. It needs only one or two conditions in order to manifest. And if you look deeply into the garbage, you will see the flower waiting to manifest again.

So the Buddhist answer to the question is that the egg is there in the chicken, and the chicken is there in the egg. No after. No before.

INTERBEING

PREPARATION: Bring children to visit an animal shelter, if possible one that allows visitors to pet the puppies and kittens. Or, arrange for a canine visit to your classroom (ideally a rescued mixed-breed). It's also helpful have each child contemplate a picture of herself as a baby. Or you can use seeds and adapt the interbeing discussion accordingly.

We are going to pet the puppy or kitten, but before we do, would you like to bow to it?

[*Yes*]

Why?

[*To show it we know it has Buddha nature; to show our love and respect to it*]

Ask the children to notice what sounds the puppies or kittens make. Our children decided their meows and barks were bells of mindfulness. Demonstrate the best way to pet the animal: bow to it, then tenderly support it with one hand under its body. Invite children to bow to, and gently pet, the puppy or kitten. Allow the children time to enjoy holding, petting, and talking to the animals. Return the animals to their baskets or resting places.

Where did the puppy come from?

[*Its mom*]

Was the puppy born?

[*Yes*]

Was it born when it came out of its mother?

[*Yes*]

I don't think so! Being born means from nothing we become something. Was the puppy nothing before it came out of its mom?

[*No . . . it was alive inside of its mom*]

We've discovered that it is not exactly correct to say that the puppy was born when it came out of its mother's womb because we know that it was alive inside of her already. Can we say that the puppy was alive before it was inside of its mother's tummy?

[*Yes*]

Can we say that it was partly alive in its mom and partly alive in its dad?

[*Yes!*]

Do you think that is true of people, too? Let's look at ourselves. Ask each child to look at their own picture as a baby. *When is your birthday?* Give children time to say their birthday.

Why do you call that your birthday?

[*Because that is the day I came out of my mom*]

If we say that we are born on the day we come out of our moms, it's like saying the puppies were born on the day they came out of their moms. And we know that's not true.

Were you nothing before you came out of your mom?

[*"No! I was alive when I was inside my mom." "My mom said she could hear me and feel me move when I was inside of her."*]

What were you before you were alive in your mom? Were you nothing?

[*"No! I was an idea waiting to happen!" "I was a little egg." "I was never nothing!"*]

So where were you before you were in your mom?

[*"Part of me was inside my mom and part was inside my dad." "I was in my grandparents." "Hey! This could go back forever!"*]

We can see that you have never been nothing! Because 'being born' means from nothing we become something . . . looking deeply, we can say that, like the puppy, we have never been born! Or maybe we can say that we have always been born. We have always been something; we have never been nothing.

Sometimes we have been an idea; sometimes we have been a part of other people; sometimes we are who we are right now. Maybe we have even been a cloud or a flower or a river. Our teacher Thich Nhat Hanh says that the day we call our birthday might be better called our Continuation Day. Why do you think he offers us that idea?

[*"To remind us that we have never been born." "We have always come from something." "We are continuing what our ancestors were continuing!"*]

Next time you have a birthday party, you might invite your friends to sing Happy Continuation Day to You! The children might want to sing the adapted Happy Birthday song to each other. *If you have never been born, can you die?*

[*No!*]

How is it that you can stay alive? How is it possible that you never die?

[*"Because you know me, I am an idea inside of you. As long as you are alive I am alive, so I will be alive in everyone you ever knew!" "When I have children, I will be a part of them." "Am I alive in everything?! I guess I am!" "Hey! This goes forward forever!"*]

Why is it important to know that we have never been born and we can never die?

[*"Because if you get sick and go to the hospital, and they tell you that you are going to die, you can say 'I will never die'; and when your family comes and they are sad you can say 'Don't be sad; I will never die.'" "Because if someone tells you that you're going to die, you won't be afraid because you'll know it's not true." "Because when we know we are alive in other people, we will take care of them better." "And we need to take care of ourselves, too, because if my friend is alive in me, then when I take care of myself, I'm taking care of her, too!"*]

So knowing that we have never been born and that we will never die keeps us from being sad, keeps us from being afraid, gives us a way to comfort our friends and family, reminds us to take care of others because we are in them and reminds us to take care

> TRACK 29
>
> No Coming,
> No Going

of ourselves because others are alive in us. Knowing we have never been born and that we will never die helps us to be happy and helps us to make others happy. Let's sing the song "No Coming, No Going" together.

resources

You can cut out or copy the
guided Pebble Meditation
cards on the following pages.

Using the Meditation Cards

- Find a quiet spot
- Sit in a comfortable position
- Sit with your back straight and shoulders
                                    relaxed

- Notice your in- and out-breath
- Pick a card
- Read slowly, so the image sinks in

- Close your eyes
- Say silently to yourself the keywords
      for each IN BREATH and OUT BREATH
- Enjoy the feeling and smile
- Take about ten breaths
      for each card

Breathing in, I see myself
   as a flower, a human flower ~

Breathing out, I am
   beautiful, just as I am
and I feel very fresh

in breath: FLOWER   out breath: FRESH

Breathing in, I see myself as a mountain ~
Breathing out,   I feel solid,
nothing can   move or
                                    distract me

in breath: MOUNTAIN   out breath: SOLID

Breathing in, I see myself as
still water, a calm, clear lake ~
Breathing out, I reflect things

just as they are,

inside and around me

in breath: STILL WATER   out breath: REFLECTING

Breathing in, I see myself as the
big blue sky, with a lot of space
in and around me ~
Breathing out, I feel very free
and at ease

in breath: SPACE   out breath: FREE

Sample Mindfulness Resources

It is helpful to find a meaningful way to start and end each session that the kids will remember and enjoy. Being aware of their breathing as they listen to the bell is a good practice. Remind them they can always return to their breathing on their own whenever they need centering. Once the children have learned to invite the bell, allow them to begin and end each of the following sessions by inviting the bell. Here are sample 45 minute–1 hour lessons for children ages 6 to 12 (more are on the Planting Seeds website):

Lesson One: Breathing with the Bell to Calm the Mind

MATERIALS: bell, glass vase, water, colored sand

1   Introduce the meaning of the bell *(page 65)* and counting the breath with the bell *(page 68)* **10 minutes.**
2   Learning to invite the bell *(page 70)* **10 minutes**
3   Mind in a Jar *(page 18)* **20 minutes**

HOMEWORK: Choose one sound or one thing that will be a bell of mindfulness for your students until the next class. When the children are in touch with that sound or thing, they stop and return to their breathing. They can also be aware of one action they do throughout the day, like putting on their backpack, opening a book, drinking, or going to the toilet. At the next class the children can share with each other how it was to do this one activity mindfully.

Lesson Two: Fresh, Solid, Calm, Free

MATERIALS: a copy of the Pebble Meditation practice sheet for each child (or give each child a blank sheet of paper so they can make their own)

1   Teach the song "Breathing In, Breathing Out" *(page 81)* **5 minutes**
2   Pebble Meditation *(page 77)* including time for sharing and reflection afterwards **15 minutes**
3   Pebble Meditation practice sheet *(page 85)* **15 minutes**

HOMEWORK: Find a space in your house where you can go to be calm. Put your pebbles there. Add anything else to your special breathing space that makes it beautiful and inviting. Tell us about it the next time we gather together.

Lesson Three: Interbeing

MATERIALS: a raisin for each child, paper, drawing supplies

1   Raisin Meditation *(page 147)* **10 minutes** or Contentment *(page 174)* **10 minutes**
2   Drawing Interbeing *(page 150)* **20 minutes**
3   Marble Roll *(page 156)*, Knee Sit, or Human Knot Game (see the Planting Seeds website for a description of the last two games) **10 minutes**

HOMEWORK: Make and serve a snack at home for your family. Share together about how the snack is interconnected with everything else.

Lesson Four: Understanding and Compassion

MATERIALS: a copy of the Two Promises Practice Sheet for each child

1   *The Two Promises* song *(page 136)* **5 minutes**
2   Sharing about the Two Promises *(page 135)* **20 minutes**
3   Two Promises Practice Sheet*(page 139–140)* **10 minutes**
4   Bowing *(page 114)* **5 minutes**

HOMEWORK: Learn the "Two Promises" song. Make up a dance for it on your own or in groups. Teach us the dance when we get together again. Or, practice understanding and compassion with someone or something, and share about it when we meet next.

Lesson Five: Touching the Earth

1   Tell the Story of Buddha and Mara *(page 123)* **10 minutes**
2   Practice Touching the Earth *(page 119)* **10 minutes**
3   What Am I Made of? *(page 127)* **30 minutes**

HOMEWORK: Spend time in nature (a park, a garden, near a tree, or with a plant). Contemplate how we are connected to this aspect of nature. Practice Asking Nature's Permission*(page 161)*

Sample Schedule for a Morning with Teens

Monastics were invited to offer a morning of mindfulness at a high school in Waldbrol, Germany. Here's the schedule of activities:

1   Awareness of Breathing (Awareness of the Length of Our In- and Out-breath, *page 68*) **5 minutes**

2   Introductions, sharing our goals for the morning **20 minutes**

3   Teaching on the benefits of mindfulness and how we can apply it in our life **20 minutes**

4   Mindful movements **10 minutes**[*]

5   Deep Relaxation *(page 89)* **30 minutes** (You can begin with a short sharing about what we do when we feel stressed.)

6   Tea and Tangerine Meditation (like Raisin Meditation) *(pages 144, 147)* **30 minutes**

7   Break **20 minutes**

8   Teaching on Deep Listening and Loving Speech **10 minutes**

9   Practice of Deep Listening in Pairs *(page 195)* **30 minutes**

10 Closing: feedback from the day, what the students liked, didn't like, what they learned **30 minutes**

Sample Schedule for a Family Day of Mindfulness

You can organize a Family Day of Mindfulness in which parents and children are together the whole day. The following schedule has been quite successful:

9:30 a.m. Arrival with an introduction to the day.

10:00 a.m. Dharma Adventure! Break into 5 groups of 5 to 10 people each,

[*] See http://vimeo.com/4853147 for a video demonstration of the 10 movements, or interbeing.org.uk/manual for a written description with drawings.

made up of adults and children. Each group goes to visit a different station to practice either Pebble Meditation *(page 77)*, making a collective artwork or nature mandala *(page 165)*, playing a cooperative game (choose one you like from Chapter Eight), making and eating a snack *(page 144)*, or engaging in role-playing games about family life *(page 194)*. Every 30 minutes the groups switch, so that each group can attend all 5 activities. Facilitators who have prepared their activities in advance stay put at their station, guiding each new group in the same activity. (Feel free to adapt the number of activities and their content to suit your group.)

12:30 p.m. Lunch

2:00 p.m. Deep Relaxation for Young People *(page 89)* guided by children, followed by Touching the Earth for Young People *(page 119)*. (This can also be read by the children).

3:00 p.m. Children and parents practice Beginning Anew *(page 51)*. (Children don't need to make cards. They can simply share their gratitude for parents. Parents collect things from nature to give to their children.)

4:00 p.m. Good-byes

SONGS

1. **I FOLLOW MY BREATH** 2:57
Jerusha (Harriet Korim Arnoldi)
from her 2011 CD, *The Stars Are Out All Day*

2. **GATHA FOR LISTENING TO THE BELL** :25
traditional gatha

3. **THE ISLAND WITHIN** :50
lyrics by Thich Nhat Hanh
music by Joseph Emet

4. **LISTEN, LISTEN** 4:46
lyrics by Thich Nhat Hanh
music by David & Tamara Hauze
from their 2011 CD, *I Have Arrived*

5. **PEBBLE MEDITATION** 7:36
read by Sister Jewel

6. **BREATHING IN, BREATHING OUT** 1:43
lyrics by Thich Nhat Hanh
music by Betsy Rose

7. **DEEP RELAXATION FOR YOUNG PEOPLE** 16:36
read by Sister Jewel

8. **IN, OUT, DEEP, SLOW** :37
lyrics by Thich Nhat Hanh
music by Chan Hoa Lam

9. **LULLABY** 1:50
Sr. True Vow

10. **PEACEFULLY FREE** 1:25
Sr. Morning Light

11. **KINDNESS** 1:44
Jamie Rusek, from her 2007 CD, *Cultivate Joy*

12. **WALK IN THE LIGHT** 1:08
traditional

13. **END OF DEEP RELAXATION** :46

14. **WALKING MEDITATION** 1:25
Sr. Khe Nghiem

15. **MAY THE DAY BE WELL** 1:26
(fun version)
Deborah Barbe

16   **WATERING SEEDS OF JOY**   3:01
lyrics by Thich Nhat Hanh
music by Sr. True Vow

17   **TOUCHING THE EARTH FOR YOUNG PEOPLE**   7:38
read by Sister Jewel

18   **GATHA FOR PLANTING A TREE**   1:41
lyrics by Thich Nhat Hanh
music adapted by Joseph Emet
from a Gao Ming Temple chant

19   **THERE'S OL' BUDDHA**   2:09
Rev. Patricia Dai-En Bennage

20   **THE TWO PROMISES**   1:39
lyrics by Plum Village
music by Betsy Rose

21   **I LOVE NATURE**   3:30
Joe Reilly, from his 2007 CD,
Children of the Earth,

22   **CONTEMPLATIONS AT MEALTIME**   1:09

23   **MANY HANDS**   3:04
Rev. Jody Kessler, from her
2003 CD, *Bare Bones*

24   **LITTLE TOMATO**   3:08
Joe Reilly, from his 2009 CD,
Touch the Earth

25   **STANDING LIKE A TREE**   :26
lyrics and music by Betsy Rose
adapted by Plum Village

26   **HAPPINESS IS HERE AND NOW**   :58
Eveline Beumkes

27   **GREAT BIG SMILE**   2:16
Gregg Hill & Jamie Rusek

28   **FEELINGS GATHA**   1:21
traditional gatha

29   **NO COMING, NO GOING**   1:00
Sr. True Virtue

LYRICS

in alphabetical order by title

Where chords are not specified, please follow the chord pattern from the previous lines.

6 BREATHING IN, BREATHING OUT

lyrics by Thich Nhat Hanh
music by Betsy Rose

        C   Am
Breathing in, breathing out . . . *(2x)*
    Dm   G
I am blooming as a flower.
    Dm G7   C
I am fresh as the dew.
      Em   Am
I am solid as a mountain.
    Dm   G Am G/B
I am firm as the Earth.
     Am G/B C
I am free.

Breathing in, breathing out . . . *(2x)*
I am water reflecting what is real,
    what is true.
And I feel there is space deep inside
    of me.
      C   F   C
I am free, I am free, I am free.

28 FEELINGS GATHA

traditional gatha

Feelings come and go like clouds in a
    windy sky.
Conscious breathing is my anchor.

. . . .

2 GATHA FOR LISTENING TO THE BELL

traditional gatha

C   G   C
Listen, listen . . . This wonderful sound
    Dm   C   G7
is bringing me back to my true home.
C   G   C
Listen, listen . . . This wonderful sound
    Dm   C   F G C
is bringing me back to my true home.

18 GATHA FOR PLANTING A TREE

lyrics by Thich Nhat Hanh
music adapted by Joseph Emet
from a Gao Ming Temple chant

    G   Em   Am   G
I entrust myself, I entrust myself
    Em   Bm
(to the Earth, to the Earth,
    C   G   D   G
and it entrusts itself to me).

to the Buddha, to the Buddha,
   and he entrusts himself to me.
to the Dharma, to the Dharma,
   and it entrusts itself to me.
to the Sangha, to the Sangha,
   and she entrusts herself to me.

27 GREAT BIG SMILE

by Gregg Hill & Jamie Rusek

G   C   F   C
I am a bird, a beautiful bird.
        G   F   C
I am the sun, the golden sun.
        G   Am   Em
I am the wind blowing in
              C   F
the beautiful bird in the sun.
        C   G   C
We are one in a wonderful world.

I am a seed, a tiny seed.
I am the rain, gentle rain.
I am a stream carrying
the tiny seed in the rain
as we change in a wonderful world.

I am a note, a simple note.
I am a song, a peaceful song.
I am a child, great big smile.
(I'm a note in a song, sing along in a
   wonderful world.)

26 HAPPINESS IS HERE AND NOW

by Eveline Beumkes

G   Bm   Em Am
Happiness is here and now. I have
            D
dropped my worries.
C   G   Am
Nowhere to go, nothing to do, no longer
D7 G
in a hurry.
Happiness is here and now. I have
   dropped my worries.
Somewhere to go, something to do, but
   I don't need to hurry.

....

1 I FOLLOW MY BREATH

by Jerusha (Harriet Korim Arnoldi)

A7   G7   A7   G7 A7
When I'm feeling lost and lonely, and I
G7   A7   G7
don't know where to go,
I follow my breath, and my breathing
   takes me home.

Refrain: I follow my breath.

Some people call it spirit, some people
   call it soul.
I just know that there's a thing that
   keeps me whole. *Refrain*

I put my hand right on my belly,
   feel my breath go up and down,
pouring fresh air everywhere from
   my toes up to my crown. *Refrain*

Oxygen comes from the trees, from the
   grasses and the leaves,
from the ocean and the rain, blows
   through us and back again. *Refrain*

Always changing, always moving, always
   blowing in and out,
always coming, always going, that's what
   breathing's all about. *Refrain*

You can try it when you're happy, then
   you try it when you're not.
You don't have to go and find it. Breath is
   something we have got. *Refrain*

If I forget about my breath, my thoughts
   can take me far away
from what's inside and all around me in
   this moment, on this day. *Refrain*

Breathing out and breathing in, and
   knowing what you're doing when
isn't easy as it sounds, but it always calms
   me down. *Refrain*

So when I'm feeling hurt or angry, and I
   don't know where to go,
I follow my breath, and my breathing
   takes me home. *Refrain*

21 **I LOVE NATURE**
by Joe Reilly

G   C   G   D

Refrain: I love Nature. Nature is cool.
The forest is my classroom. The Earth is
   my school.
Trees are my teachers. Animals are my
   friends.

G   C   D   G

And on this school, all life depends.

G   C

I love all of Nature. Yes, it's true.

G   D

That means I love myself, and I love
   you, too.
When I look around me, Nature's all
   that I'm seeing—
plants, animals, Earth, sky, and human
   beings.
Nature is like one big community.
Many animals may live inside just
   one tree.
And that tree gives us oxygen to help
   us breathe.

D   G

This whole interaction is called ecology.
   Refrain

I love flowers. They are so pretty.
I love them in the forest and I love
   them in the city.
And I love mushrooms too on a pizza
   or in salad,
but my favorite place for mushrooms
   is right here in this love ballad.
I love children and I love H_2O.

And children who like Nature can help
   the rivers flow
by protecting habitats like wetlands
   and wet meadows.
When we work together, we can all
   help Nature grow, so: *Refrain*

So let's love Nature right now with
   all our hearts.
That's right, this present moment is
   a great place to start.
We don't need any money. It may take
   a little time.
We need to open up our arms, hearts,
   mouths, and minds
so we can see the gifts Mother Nature
   can bring.
When we learn to appreciate it, it makes
   us want to sing.
And when we are smiling and singing
   our song,
other people hear us and may want
   to sing along. They sing: *Refrain*

....

8 **IN, OUT, DEEP, SLOW**
lyrics by Thich Nhat Hanh
music by Chan Hoa Lam

G D C   G   C   G D7   G

In, out, deep, slow, calm, ease, smile, release.
Present moment, wonderful moment.

3 THE ISLAND WITHIN

lyrics by Thich Nhat Hanh
music by Joseph Emet

        Dm   Dm/C
Breathing in, I go back
      B♭   A   Dm
to the island within myself.
       F   C
There are beautiful trees within the island.
     A7   Dm
There are clear streams of water.
       B♭
There are birds, sunshine, and fresh air.
Gm   A   Dm
Breathing out, I feel safe.
  B♭   A   Dm
I enjoy going back to my island.

....

11 KINDNESS

by Jamie Rusek

What is the greatest, what is the greatest,
   what is the greatest wisdom of all? *(2x)*
Kindness, kindness, that is the greatest
   wisdom of all. *(2x)*

4 LISTEN, LISTEN

lyrics by Thich Nhat Hanh
music by David & Tamara Hauze

E7   A   E7   A
Listen, listen . . . This wonderful sound
         E7 A   E7
brings me back to my true self.

....

24 LITTLE TOMATO

by Joe Reilly

Joe:
  F#m   A
Hello little tomato,
       D
Can you tell me all the secrets of this
   life that you know?
In what type of environment did you
   grow?
Have you ever seen the city streets of
   Bordeaux?
Hello little tomato,
I'm happy to have you as part of my
   bean stew.
Again let me ask you, do you remember
   last September,
Growing together with the cucumber
   in the fall slumber?
Sometimes I wonder if it felt a little edgy
To be a young veggie before the harvest
   time.

Tomato:
Well I started out as just a seed.
when I germinated I was just a weed.

I grew up strong, my branches creeped
along.
I always hoped that one day I'd be in
a song.
But alas, I know I've digressed
Sitting in your stew you might think
I'm depressed.
But I'm quite content, and will not
prevent you from eating me.
I'm so happy to become part of you,
your thoughts and your body.
It's like one big energy exchange party.
And what, you ask, started all of this?
It was the sun and photosynthesis.
I'm a producer, you're a consumer.
I'll say it again, I was fed by the rain and
received the most from the compost.
Decomposing matter helped me grow
fatter,
More red and juicy. Now won't you
excuse me,
Its time for you to stop talking and
consume me, consume me.

Joe:
Thank you, little tomato.
There are so many more things that
I could say though.
But it's enough to say I'm grateful
For all the stuff that you're made of:
The water, the soil, and the sunshine;
The gardener who staked out your vine;
The harvester who picked you at the
right time.
I even have to acknowledge the energy
divine
That is in you and flows from you to me.
I will do my very best to live and to be

Worthy of your time and your energy.
I will eat you happily, mindfully.
Come rest for a while with me in my
belly,
Then return to the earth for another
rebirth.
I'll see you again my vegetable friend.
I'll see you again my little veggie friend.
I'll see you again.

Joe: Hello little tomato.

Tomato: Hello.

....

9 LULLABY
by Sr. True Vow

C   F
I hear you, I hear you.
Am   Dm
Have no fear, don't cry anymore.
And I'll hold you, I'll hold you
if you'll only let these arms enfold
you ('fold you).
And I love you, I love you.
I'll do my best to take good care of you.
'Cause I know you, I know you.
        Am   Dm
You're the apple of your grandmother's eye.
You're the warrior-child who's willing
to cry.
        Am
You're the lion's roar from deep down
   F G
inside . . .

23 MANY HANDS
by Rev. Jody Kessler

G C G C   D   G
On this plate there are many hands—
   C   Bm
the hands that sowed the seeds, the
Am   D
hands that plowed the land,
   G   Bm
the hands that worked the harvest,
   C   D   Em
and brought it to the stands.
   C G C   D   G
Yes, on this plate are many hands.

In this bowl are sun and rain and air,
the garden soil and all the tiny
    creatures that live there,
the delicate balance of beings great
    and small.
Yes, in this little bowl we have them all.

In this meal are many hearts and souls—
some may be our families who served
    it in our bowls
some may be migrant workers whom
    we will never know,
who can't afford to buy the food they
    grow.

In this room there are many hands.
Let's join them all together in a circle,
    if we can.
And in this sacred silence, let there be
    gratitude
for the many hearts and hands that
    made this food. *(2x)*

15 MAY THE DAY BE WELL *(fun version)*
by Deborah Barbe

           A   E
May the *(day)* be well, may the *(night)* be
    well.
             D   A
May the *(midday hour)* bring happiness, too.
                    E
In every minute and every second, may
  D   E   A
the day and night be well.

    dog, cat, human being
    sun, moon, planet Earth
    monks, nuns, our teacher, Thay
    day, night, midday hour

....

29 NO COMING, NO GOING
by Sr. True Virtue

    A   E   A
No coming, no going, no after, no before.
  D   C#m   Bm
I hold you close to me. I release you to
E   A
be so free . . .
  Bm   A   E   C#m
because I am in you, and you are in me,
  Bm   A   E   A
because I am in you, and you are in me.

10 PEACEFULLY FREE
by Sr. Morning Light

C G/B Am G C G/B   Am   G
I am   so free because I can be me.
Look at the clouds at play, passing over
   every day.
Inside, the sky so blue, immense, spacious,
   and true.

I'll be tall like the sky, wide enough to
   embrace what's inside.
Just like the clouds passing by, flying high
   in the grand-open sky.
Everything around me will be
   loved, embraced, and peacefully free.
Everything inside me will be
   loved, embraced, and peacefully free.

....

25 STANDING LIKE A TREE
lyrics and music by Betsy Rose
adapted by Plum Village

C   F
Standing like a tree with my roots
        C   F
   down deep and my branches wide
      G Am
   and o-pen . . .
Em   F
Come down the rain (come, come),
     G   C
   come down the sun,
   Em   F   G   C
return to the Earth, return to the One.
C   F   G   C

19 THERE'S OL' BUDDHA
by Rev. Patricia Dai-En Bennage

Em   Am   G
There's ol' Buddha sittin' under the bodhi
   tree (bodhi tree).
There's ol' Buddha, his mind as quiet/
   empty/peaceful as it could be (it
   could be).
Am   Em Am
Sittin' like a wise ol' frog, sittin' like a
             Em
   bump on a log,
Am   Em   C
Sittin' with a smile on his face, kinda like
      G
   empty space.
Am   Em Am   Em
Doesn't mind rain, doesn't mind thunder.
C
What could bother ol' Buddha, I wonder?

response:

                        F
He wasn't bothered by _____. He wasn't
              C   Am
   bothered by _____.
         Dm G   G7   C
He let that _____ just roll on by (just
F   G   C
roll on by).

20 THE TWO PROMISES

lyrics by Plum Village
music by Betsy Rose

    C   Am   F G C
I vow to develop understanding
                                   Am
in order to live peacefully with people,
F   G   C
animals, plants, and minerals. *(2x)*
Am Em F   C   Am G/B C G C
Mm, ah . . . Mm, ah . . . Mm,   ah.

I vow to develop my compassion
in order to protect the lives of people,
animals, plants, and minerals. *(2x)*
Mm, ah *(3x)*

....

12 WALK IN THE LIGHT

traditional

C   G/B
Walk in the light, beautiful light.
Am   G/B
Come where the dewdrops of (mercy/
    freedom) shine bright.
C   G/B
Shine (all around/on inside) us by day
    and by night.
Am   G/B   C
We are the light of the world. We are the
G   C
light of the world.

14 WALKING MEDITATION

by Sr. Khe Nghiem

C   F C G
Walking, breathing, smiling, easing . . .
C   G   F   G
stepping mindfully on the Earth,
F   C   F   C   F C
dropping all thinking, worries, and
    anxieties.
                    G   F   Am
Oh, Mother Earth, I am here . . .
Dm   Am
Brother Sky!
    C   G   F   C   G
Oh, Sister Cloud em – bra – cing . . .
    Am G/B C   F-G   C
Yes, life is here dwelling i–n freedom.

16 WATERING SEEDS OF JOY
lyrics by Thich Nhat Hanh
music by Sr. True Vow

G   C   Em   Am
My mother, my father, they are in me,
G/B   C   D   G
and when I look, I see myself in them.
The Buddha, the Patriarchs, they are in
   me,
and when I look, I see myself in them.

       C   G   C
I am a continuation of my mother and
            G
my father.
       C   G   C
I am a continuation of all my blood
G/B Am G
ancestors.
         C   G
It is my aspiration to preserve and
C   G
continue to nourish
            C   G
seeds of goodness, seeds of skill, seeds of
            C
happiness which I have inherited.
Em   Am   C   G/B
It's also my desire to recognize the seeds
         Am   Em
of fear and suff'ring I have inherited,
     Am G/B C   G   C
and, bit by   bit, to transform them . . .
       G   C
transform them.

I am a continuation of the Buddha and
   the Patriarchs.
I am a continuation of all my spiritual
   teachers.
It is my deep aspiration to preserve, develop, and nourish
                    C   G
seeds of understanding, seeds of love,
                 C
seeds of freedom which they have
                 Am
transmitted to me.

            G/B   C
In my daily life I also want to sow seeds
            G/B
of love and compassion
            Am
in my own consciousness and in the
         G/B   C
hearts of other people.
               G/B
I am determined not to water the seeds
     Am   G/B
of craving, aversion, and violence in
     C
me.
I am determined not to water the seeds
   of craving, aversion, and violence in
   others.
               G/B   Am
With resolve and with compassion, I give
     G/B   C
rise to this aspiration:
               G/B   D
May my practice be an offering of the
G
heart. *(2x)*

Resources

On the *Planting Seeds* website, www.plantingseedsbook.org, you will find many resources for your practice and further reading including a glossary and additional practices and exercises.

Acknowledgments

We wish to thank Terry Cortes-Vega and Susan Hadler for their generous time and energy in carefully reviewing many drafts of this book. Terry spent many brainstorming hours on Skype with the editor, being a very creative and supportive sounding board. We are also very grateful to Terry for the many activities and practices of her own that she contributed to the book.

We also wish to thank Meena Srinivasan for her significant contribution to the research section of Chapter One and for the voices of her students. We are deeply grateful to May Fu, Tineke Spruytenburg, Meena Srinivasan, Susanna Barkataki, Cathy Barkataki, Annie Mahon, Kathi Kollerman, Anita Wong, Ingrid Depner, Sandra Huber, and Angela Bergmann for their review of the entire manuscript or portions of it. We are also grateful to the many Sangha friends who helped transcribe talks for this book.

We are very grateful to Sr. True Vow (The Nghiem) for her dedicated and creative audio editing and arranging of the songs for the CD.

We deeply appreciate the many contributors who shared their experience and wisdom of sharing mindfulness with children.

**PARALLAX
PRESS**

Parallax Press, a nonprofit organization, publishes books on engaged Buddhism
and the practice of mindfulness by Thich Nhat Hanh and other authors.
All of Thich Nhat Hanh's work is available at our online store and
in our free catalog. For a copy of the catalog, please contact:

Parallax Press
P.O. Box 7355
Berkeley, CA 94707
Tel: (510) 525-0101
www.parallax.org

Monastics and laypeople practice the art of mindful living in the tradition of
Thich Nhat Hanh at retreat communities worldwide. To reach any of these
communities, or for information about individuals and families
joining for a practice period, please contact:

Plum Village
13 Martineau
33580 Dieulivol, France
www.plumvillage.org

Blue Cliff Monastery
3 Mindfulness Road
Pine Bush, NY 12566
www.bluecliffmonastery.org

Deer Park Monastery
2499 Melru Lane
Escondido, CA 92026
www.deerparkmonastery.org

European Institute of
Applied Buddhism
Schaumburgweg 3
51545 Waldbröl, Germany
www.eiab.eu

The Mindfulness Bell, a journal of the art of mindful living in the tradition of
Thich Nhat Hanh, is published three times a year by Plum Village. To subscribe or
to see the worldwide directory of Sanghas, visit www.mindfulnessbell.org.